TIO
BAU : FRE

STUDIES IN
POETIC DISCOURSE

MERIDIAN

Crossing Aesthetics

Werner Hamacher

& David E. Wellbery

Editors

Translated by
William Whobrey

Translations from
the French and Latin by
Bridget McDonald

*Stanford
University
Press*

---

*Stanford
California
1996*

STUDIES IN
POETIC DISCOURSE

*Mallarmé, Baudelaire,
Rimbaud, Hölderlin*

Hans-Jost Frey

Originally published in German in 1986
as *Studien über das Reden der Dichter*
by Wilhelm Fink Verlag
© 1986 by Wilhelm Fink Verlag

Stanford University Press
Stanford, California
© 1996 by the Board of Trustees of the
Leland Stanford Junior University
Printed in the United States of America

CIP data are at the end of the book

Stanford University Press publications are
distributed exclusively by Stanford University Press
within the United States, Canada, Mexico, and
Central America; they are distributed exclusively
by Cambridge University Press throughout
the rest of the world.

Contents

STUDIES IN
POETIC DISCOURSE

Foreword

READER: What is this book you've written all about?

AUTHOR: I can't explain it to you. Why don't you just read it? I said what I had to say as well as I could and I can't say it any differently now.

READER: You're not getting off the hook that easily. You claim to be a scholar of literature, and I don't think it's asking too much to ask you to explain what you're doing. What would happen if everyone just started talking without being responsible for what they said? You have to be able to explain what you're talking about and how you relate to your subject. That's the only way to create useful secondary literature.

AUTHOR: That may be true, but hopefully the damage is minimal. And besides, I'm only marginally concerned whether what I do is scholarly or not, and whether it is useful or not. Instead, . . .

READER: Do you really think that anyone would want to read your book after hearing what you just said?

AUTHOR: Whoever hears this, as you just said, has already begun to read our discussion and has therefore declared a willingness to listen to us. It may be possible to create an interest in the unexpected. Those who cling too much to their own expectations can't listen. That holds true for those who read a text for its usefulness as well.

READER: Do you want to be read the same way you read?

AUTHOR: That's not for me to say. Everyone reads the way they best know how. How do I read texts, anyway? I wanted to comment on this when you interrupted me a minute ago.

READER: That may have been for the better.

AUTHOR: Perhaps. Our relationship to a text constantly changes. You could almost say that we get closest to a text when our relationship to it seems most endangered. Finding and losing are close bedfellows in reading. The most important discovery is all the closer the less we can firmly hold on to it.

READER: That's just another one of your paradoxical formulations that sounds intellectual but doesn't help at all. Said more plainly: they remain incomprehensible.

AUTHOR: I'm sorry. I would like to speak plainly and clearly. But it's still hard for me to talk about literature. I have tried several times to say something about it in this book. In trying to understand a text, it seems to me that the question of my relationship to a text, for example, is a question manifest in the text itself.

READER: Not a very original thought! Nonscholarly readers have always tried to insert their own questions into the text. The text as a mirror, as the forest that echoes what is shouted into it and that can't be seen anymore for all the trees.

AUTHOR: What you're describing is appropriation. If we read this way, we reduce the text to ourselves. It fulfills our own expectations in that we find in it what we already have. But I'm talking about something else when I say that the question of my relationship to a text is the same as the question of the text itself. A text is discourse, and I speak about it. By speaking about it, I do what I am speaking about, and therefore, whenever I speak about a text, I also speak about what I'm doing. The question of my relationship to a text is always the question of my relationship to my own speaking about it.

READER: If that's your question, then it's a long way from being the text's question, which, after all, doesn't concern itself with other texts.

AUTHOR: Perhaps it does, if whatever is said always means something. But I'm really concerned about something else. Imagine that you're riding on a train. Most of the seats are occupied, and the people are talking. No matter why they're traveling, people always have something to say that they think is important and that they think other people have to know about. They are completely engrossed in what they are doing, and they speak with a single purpose, just like the train staying on the tracks. You sit there and listen because you can't do anything else. But suddenly you stop listening. You don't hear what the people are saying, but only that they are talking. And you notice that they only talk so much and so loud and for so long, because they aren't aware of what they're doing. They don't even notice that they're talking. They're much too caught up in what they're saying. But you sit there and hear talking, without paying attention to what's being said, and wait for the train to derail. You feel like a rock on the tracks.

READER: I really don't know what you're talking about anymore.

AUTHOR: Then we have reached our destination—literature, I mean, a speaking that is no longer concerned just with what is being said, but with itself. Authors are conscious of the fact that they are speaking. This kind of discourse need not concern itself only with speaking, and even if speaking becomes a topic, we fail to exercise any control over it, since discourse is something that only exists through speaking. We have to speak to have discourse. Even if you sit silently in the train and only listen, discourse takes place inside you. If you listen in a way that what is said is less important than the speaking itself, then you are listening literarily, and you speak literarily whenever you are aware that what you say is being spoken. You will then speak differently and speak about different things. Literature is, among other things, the admission of its own linguistic nature. This is why politicians' speeches are not literature, even though they could be read in a literary manner, something that would not necessarily increase their effectiveness.

READER: Now I see what you're getting at. If literature concerns itself not only with communicating this or that but also with discourse, something that makes communication possible in the first place, then it develops a relationship to itself that is similar to the relationship that you have to it. You are concerned with a discourse that is concerned with itself. In this way, you find your relationship to a text within the text itself.

AUTHOR: That's pretty good. But now the difficulties involved in my relationship to my own discourse and that of others start to become clear. If both are concerned with discourse, that is to say, with themselves, how can they be kept apart?

READER: The literary text is not concerned with itself the same way you are. It is a self-referential discourse, whereas you say this or that about it as self-referential discourse. Why can't speaking *about* the text be considered instrumental discourse?

AUTHOR: I thought I had already answered that. But perhaps this is one of those questions that must constantly be asked without ever being answered. Whenever I talk about literature, I am concerned not with a discourse that says something but that says itself, that is, a noninstrumental discourse that goes beyond its own subject. An instrumental speaking about literature would be a discourse that remained completely untouched by the insight that causes it to be communicated to begin with, even though such an insight opens up the possibility of a discourse that is both objective and self-referential. How can I speak about the self-referentiality of discourse and at the same time forget that I'm speaking?

READER: That doesn't seem to me to be so improbable, if you allow me to follow your train of thought for a minute, but seems unavoidable. Why do you even want to talk about the special relationship of discourse to what is spoken and to itself? Only because literature doesn't explicitly talk about this relationship itself, and because it couldn't possibly do so, because it is it. To describe this relationship, you have to be able to keep your distance to it. You might not be speaking literarily, but it then becomes possible to speak of the literary. But that's only something I read in your book.

AUTHOR: That won't stop me from contradicting you. Your solution is a weak compromise in which literary discourse is unable to speak about what it is in order to be literature, whereas speaking about literature avoids being literature in order to be able to say what it is. I'm afraid I can't be that easily appeased. Can't we imagine a speaking about literature that is itself literature?

READER: A literature that says what it is? Now you're asking me to do more than you yourself have done. Why don't we just trade roles? It would be fun to be an author. You're imagining some kind of literature that would no longer require any secondary literature, because it could say everything itself. Or said another way: secondary literature would be the highest form of literature both by being self-referential discourse and still being able to speak. This utopia is just too imprecise. The way your question is worded, it can only be answered with yes. Nothing prevents speaking about literature from being literary discourse . . .

AUTHOR: If that's the case, then we can do away with literary criticism. Literature is all we need.

READER: . . . but speaking about literature is not literature. You said that literary discourse always says something but is at the same time concerned with itself. A literary discourse is possible whose subject is the self-reference of literary discourse. But this spoken self-reference does not communicate the special way in which that special discourse refers to itself. This reference presents itself as the discourse that speaks of self-reference. But the premise of what is said within this discourse remains out of reach and unspeakable. It is possible to talk about the self-reference of literary discourse, and it is possible to express how discourse refers to itself in a text, but no discourse can accomplish this on its own, because it always exists as something greater than what it is able to say. All discourse would require interpretation if we want to understand how a text speaks about itself through itself. But this is not always a beneficial undertaking. Literature on literature: perhaps these are texts in which what is spoken can be read as a figure for its being spoken. Texts like those that have engaged your efforts. Interpretation—what I read your book to mean—is the attempt to recognize the figure as such and thereby to resolve it, so that it is applied to the unique way in which a special text constitutes discourse as self-reference.

AUTHOR: I'm grateful to you for this somewhat tedious production that I encouraged you to pursue. Now I have a better understanding of the kinds of texts I have written about, and how everything that is written relies on the reader. Would you mind if I used our discussion as a foreword to my book?

READER: I prefer the middleword or nowword to the foreword or afterword.

AUTHOR: Sayings like that guarantee an effective ending. But they are less effective than one might hope. There really isn't anything that can be said against what you've just said, but the fact that you have said it allows it to become what it would least like to be: the foreword or afterword.

H.-J. F.

Mallarmé

THE UNDECIDABILITY OF TEXTS

According to an often professed characteristic of literary discourse, expression cannot be separated from its being expressed. This inseparability of being expressed and expression, if it is to be taken seriously, precludes all attempts at determining a text's meaning and at making this meaning available to others. The burgeoning business of meaning determination, which to some extent always lives off the claim of saying the same thing but in a different, better, simpler, clearer way, runs the risk of atrophy. What remains is the task of reading texts differently from the way in which communications are received. Texts cannot be understood if we stop short at a presumed meaning. They must be allowed to continue their discourse. Only when they continue speaking can they survive as the expression of what has been expressed and as the irreducible relationship between the two. A reader is not primarily a receiver of content. A reader enables a text to speak. This is quickly forgotten, however, if the reader is too intent on discovering what the text has to say. Hunger for information is deadly to language. Information always attempts to suppress language in favor of what it can convey. Literature is created when we realize that information is dependent on language. By contrast, if we imagine what is expressed to be the thing itself, forgetting its dependence on language, then referential illusion takes over. This can be observed in the most elementary form of linking expression to expressing, whenever everything that is expressed is represented only by its having been expressed. No human discourse can, by itself, prove the existence of what it says. The potential for lying is based on the fact that discourse alone cannot verify an extralinguistic reference. Whether someone is telling the truth or not cannot be determined by discourse, and the smooth flow of the exchange of utterances in human intercourse is based not on the recognizable truthfulness of the utterances but either on a mutual trust that grants the discourse partner some degree of trustworthiness or on the fact that the referential illusion has become a convention.

If referential illusion is the assumption that whatever is expressed has some extralinguistic correspondence, then simply ignoring this correspondence cannot result in unveiling the illusion, since by doing so we would fall prey to the object of investigation. The illusion is not based on assuming an extralinguistic reference but rather on overlooking the uncertainty of this assumption. The simple negation of this assumption would lead to the same mistake. It is therefore impossible to come to grips with referential illusion by asserting a lack of referentiality. The realization that texts are undecidable is the only solution. What is expressed remains linked to discourse, not because there is no correspondence outside of discourse, but because it is uncertain whether or not these correspondences exist. Certainty about what is expressed exists only within the discourse in which it is expressed and only for as long as it remains dependent on the fact that it was spoken. This limitation of expression to the discourse that transmits it contradicts a common, even dominant concept of language as an instrument of mediation, leading to the assumption that what is expressed exists outside of language before and after its transmission and is therefore no longer something that is expressed but an extralinguistic given. Language is degraded to an available means, used whenever needed. But suppression of the importance of discourse as such does not extinguish that importance. Discourse is allowed instead to break out all the stronger in other ways. Whoever believes that language is an instrument believes that he can control it and use it in any way he desires. But in refusing to acknowledge the dependence of what is expressed on its being expressed, he subjects himself to the effects of discourse without being able to defend himself against it. He is dominated by discourse because he is vulnerable to everything it says without considering its linguistic status. Given that the utterance gains such power as soon as it is forgotten, it is not redundant to speak about it in terms of itself. Literature is this kind of discourse.

Whatever literature may be cannot be determined from its contents. It is less an arbitrary speaking about special things than a special speaking about arbitrary things. Literature is a manner of speaking. It speaks in such a way that it contradicts referential illusion. A literary text is never primarily information, but discourse. This is not to say that this discourse remains within itself and says nothing, but that it works against the tendency to decouple the expressed from the being expressed, and that, by saying what it says, always reminds us both of itself and the foundation of the expressed. By always drawing attention to itself as discourse and thereby to the linguistic foundation of what is expressed, literature attains the power that other forms of discourse claim to have when speaking beyond themselves and over themselves. It is less mystified and mystifies less. Sometimes literature suffers from being itself by denying itself the chance of having any direct effect. If it becomes untrue to itself, then it loses itself. If literature remains true to itself, then the chorus of ephemeral voices refuses to take it seriously. This does not compromise literature's importance, however, because when literature is taken seriously, it is misunderstood. Literature's task is to question the fact that what is expressed is always taken seriously, a fact that characterizes everyday relations between people. This questioning reveals the unbreakable link of what is expressed to its being expressed. This can only take place by putting obstacles in the way of referential reading, making it more difficult for what is expressed to transcend discourse. Literature is reserved. It avoids assertions or identifies them as such. It does not easily grant meaning from within itself but offers several meanings

without enabling a choice between them. Since literary texts are
undecidable, they remain present in speaking, and they speak
continuously. Their reservedness is the reserve from which they
draw the strength to have meaning and out of which they never
really lose themselves if their message is not to fall silent.

The opinion that texts are not reliable, namely when answers,
not questions, deeds, not words, are called for, has to do with their
reservedness. But too many evil deeds take place in the name of a
discourse that is taken seriously to justify ignoring discourses that
do not claim to take themselves seriously. If taking seriously what is
expressed equates to suppressing its language, then literature de-
serves to be taken seriously as a disruption of seriousness, but in
such a way that it questions itself as well. This is prompted by texts
that do not allow themselves to be pushed into the backwater of
undecidability. The suspension of information characterized by the
insolubility between expressing and expression is disrupted by the
fact that extralinguistic reference is absent not because it does not
exist, but because we cannot know whether it exists or not. A
literary text is not a text that has no reference but a text whose
referentiality is uncertain. Therefore literature should not be misunderstood as a speaking that is satisfied with the irreducible
language of what it says. In its undecidedness, it talks about
whether its saying is the only reason for what it has expressed, or
whether this has any correspondence that would allow a transcendence of language. Literature is not only a speaking that cannot be
founded in the extralinguistic, but it also fails to recognize this
impossibility. It is therefore not enough to say that the literary
exists within the insoluble relation between expressing and expression or in the transcendence of referential illusion. The literary also
refuses to be satisfied with this definition. Literature distances itself
from itself and finds itself through self-denial. The literary is
therefore not accessible through a theory that could define it as
what it is. Literature always questions whatever it threatens to
become, not to negate it but to bring it back to undecidability. The
undecidable text has an undefinable status, because it constantly

calls itself into question. The doubt in referentiality is always preferable to referential illusion, especially when it counts.

Mallarmé's texts distinguish themselves by a particularly high degree of restraint. They are never informative and don't present themselves as what they seem to say. Since they don't communicate anything tangible, they are considered to be dark. Where darkness is a reproach, the concept of language as means predominates. Whoever speaks darkly does not know how to use language properly and therefore expresses himself unclearly. Clarity is defined as the flawless transmission of a message. If discourse had no other function than to act as a transmitter, then it could properly be found lacking. There is, however, a kind of restraint with regard to communication that is not lacking. The darkness of discourse, the fact that it does not directly lead to something definite, counters referential illusion and moves discourse itself into the spotlight. This is discourse's own clarity, lacking in communication that merely seeks to inform, remaining hidden from itself in shadows of self-deception. Because darkness disrupts direct communication, it blocks the unambiguous path of communications and creates a realm where discourse is freed from its instrumental bonds.

Communications are disrupted if what is being communicated is uncertain, that is, when a single meaning is lost and the multiple meanings of the dark text challenge the linearity of discourse. Ambiguous discourse leads to a fork in the road with several options. It is impossible to choose between them because each is the right one and none can be ignored. For Mallarmé the image of a bifurcated fish tail sometimes represents the suspension of this hopeless uncertainty. It appears in his *Coup de dés* (Throw of the dice) in connection with the indecisive Hamlet figure as the "impatient final bifurcated flakes" (*Oeuvres complètes*, 470) and is always meant wherever sirens surface or disappear. In the prose *Solitude*, the fish tail characterizes indeterminate discourse and becomes a metaphor for undecidability. "When a speaker affirms, in one sense more than its opposite, an aesthetic opinion, generally beyond eloquence, which seduces, the result is nonsense because under sinuous and contradictory blows to the rump, it is not at all unhappy to end in a fish tail; only refuses that this be displayed and spread around like a public phenomenon" (408).

Mallarmé distinguishes between the assertion of an opinion that leads to something stupid and the idea that brings oppositions together, terminating in a fish tail that points to unavoidable duality. The impossibility of taking one path or the other obviates the requirement to choose one over the other. Opinionated discourse is instrumental because it serves as a means of saying something to someone. This scheme of communications is challenged as soon as the message can no longer be linked to a point of view, which is to say, to a speaker. All opinion depends on a point of view, thereby rejecting undecidability. The opinionated decide when no decision can be made. This results in absurdity ("the result is nonsense"). The word *défalquer*, "to cut off with a sickle," points to the absurdity inherent in cutting off one end of the fish tail, that is, in the decision that enables the assertion of an opinion. The decision is a mutilation of the undecidable idea, which can only be determined in one particular direction if the opposing direction is suppressed. The problem of ambiguity cannot be solved by force. The decision must be suspended between the available possibilities, and the discourse that cannot be attached to one or another meaning must remain suspended. This suspension of discourse is a darkness grounded in undecidability. To characterize the discourse that cannot be determined, Mallarmé uses the concept of vagueness. In a late poem, we read: "Le sens trop précis rature / Ta vague littérature" (The too precise meaning, erases / Your vague literature [73]). In the contrast between vagueness and precision, the metaphor of cutting off, also present in the etymology of decision (*décision*), is effective. Precision destroys vagueness by surrounding it with clear, cutting lines. The limits of the precise and unequivocal seek to protect it from the limitlessness of vague ambiguity. Turned around, the opening to vagueness renounces an aesthetic that could define works of art as final forms. Vague discourse hovers in language, by which it is carried and which it employs. It does not rush purposefully toward a statement but remains suspended in the tension between expressing and expression, in which it receives itself as a potential of the statement.

Vagueness is an unsatisfying condition because the possibilities of discourse are blurred by undifferentiation. Insofar as the experience of vagueness is equivalent to the experience of lost differentiation, there always exists within it the desire to break out. If ambiguity is recognized as irreducible, then it is so only through a differentiation that is not also a decision. The end of Mallarmé's sentence, in which he refuses to spread out the fish tail and display it publicly, seems, however, to reject any such attempt. It is not enough to renounce the reduction of ambiguity by choosing one or the other meaning, but it is also not enough to want to spread out ambiguity through the display of individual meanings. This kind of spreading out and rolling up (*dérouler*, *étaler*) is only made possible by sacrificing the simultaneity of meanings. As meanings in the clarifying dissection of vagueness are presented, one after the other, ambiguous discourse is transformed into a series of single meanings. Every single phase of this series is an equally inadmissable and unavoidable determination of the undecidable and therefore, if only temporarily, a precise reduction that can only be challenged in the next phase of the unfurling process, in turn subject to the same indictment. The unfurling of the simultaneous within the sequential makes different meanings available, but it also invalidates ambiguity because it is not a succession but a coincidence of meanings. Mallarmé refuses to unfurl the fish tail because a list of meanings would destroy the many possibilities of vagueness. This presents what might be unavoidable in the attempt to explain a dark text. It seems unavoidable to take apart what is in simultaneity still rolled into one. We must ask ourselves, however, what essential part of the ambiguous text is lost in the transformation of the simultaneous to the sequential. If nothing were to be lost, then the clear text could easily replace the dark text, whose darkness becomes nothing more than a reparable deficiency. If darkness is necessary, however, then it must be understood as such, as something that never can be translated into clarity. The transformation of the simultaneous into the sequential opens itself to the accusation of being a reduction of the ambiguity of the text, from whose recognition it proceeded in the first place. As soon as unfurling the meanings of a text is understood to be a reductive act, then one must be able to show in what way this act misses the text. It should therefore be possible to grasp the irreducibility of the ambiguous text in its positivity.

Something always remains unspoken in ambiguous discourse. It does not unfurl itself and therefore always contains more than it specifically states. Discourse restrains itself in indecision, which is not just insufficiency, because it is only made possible by the fact that a decision is absent. The totality of unrealized possibilities is the prerequisite for the decision that destroys the indecision upon which it relies. Both relate to each other as actuality toward virtuality. Decision makes actuality possible but also destroys all possibilities brought together in virtuality aside from the one that was chosen. Thus decision is always impoverishment. Speaking, however, is deciding. Whoever speaks says something to the exclusion of everything else. If ambiguity eliminates the decisiveness of discourse, then virtuality is preserved in actuality by ambiguous discourse. Ambiguity is the actualization of virtuality as virtuality. This actualized virtuality is incapable of being a statement in which it would simultaneously be nullified. It is accessible as the unspoken within the ambiguous discourse in which the statement is suspended. This accessibility of the unspoken is difficult to understand. It must be connected to the way in which the ambiguity is experienced. This cannot occur in a way that allows for different ways of reading a text, since this would mean that what may not occur has already occurred. When we read a discourse twice, the unfurling of the ambiguous text into a sequence of singular meanings would already have taken place, by which the undecided balance, the main element of ambiguity, would migrate to the poles between which the ambiguity hangs suspended. If there is to be another way of experiencing ambiguity, then it must precede any such unfurling and allow for the simultaneous acceptance of a plurality while recognizing the singular sequence of words. The ambiguity that lies in the unviolated unity of discourse is its density. The experience of the density of a text is the motivation for the analytical explication of meanings. The varied meanings are present in the experience of ambiguity as density, but this unity makes it impossible to separate the different levels of meaning. The undecidability of meanings in the experience of density is the same vagueness that Mallarmé claims for literature. If density is experienced independently of the unfurling of ambiguity, then it is something more than the sum of distinguishable meanings. Density is what is unspoken in discourse, where virtuality is constantly effective as an unyielding foundation and as the eternal fountain of meaning, beyond grasp in individual meanings and their sum. The force of meaning is most active when it does not rest in the acquired meaning but when it can be read as an eternal promise. This promise lies in the irretrievable deferment of the spoken in the clarity of undecidable speaking.

The dense text is not explainable, because any explanation is a dilution of the density and thereby misses its mark. Understanding in literature is not the determination of meaning, because ambiguity prevents discourse from ever being replaced by something that has been determined from it. In every attempt to fix discourse to this or that possible meaning, we are thrown back to the discourse itself, which will not allow itself to be reduced. Discourse is ambiguous not because it means more than one thing, but because it presents itself as the potential of its own meaning. The power of discourse lies not in what it expresses but in its speaking. An unresolvable tension exists between the two, by which speaking manifests itself as the unspeakable potential of what has been spoken. The unspoken part of discourse is what makes it possible to say anything at all. But discourse as its own unspoken is made accessible in the multiplicity of meanings as its inexpressible simultaneity. Discourse speaks in undecidable ambiguity, always focused not only on the external or what is to be expressed but also on itself as the source of all that is expressed. Mallarmé says that in poetry the initiative is given to words (366). This is to say that they are no longer used by someone to communicate something already known but begin to gush out. Out of their relationship to each other, words gain the ability to pour out their hidden and repressed potential for meaning. The texts that allow this force of words to be active are no longer unequivocal or equivocal, meaning this or that. They are carried by the pure ability of words to have meaning. Speaking regains its virtuality through them (368).

THE FOAM

A la nue accablante tu
Basse de basalte et de laves
A même les échos esclaves
Par une trompe sans vertu

Quel sépulcral naufrage (tu
Le sais, écume, mais y baves)
Supréme une entre les épaves
Abolit le mât dévêtu

Ou cela que furibond faute
De quelque perdition haute
Tout l'abîme vain éployé

Dans le si blanc cheveu qui traîne
Avarement aura noyé
Le flanc enfant d'une sirène.

By the crushing cloud stilled
Shoal of basalt and lava
Down even with the enslaved echoes
By a trumpet without force

What sepulchral wreck (you
Know, foam, but babble there)
Supreme, one among the derelicts
Abolished the stripped mast

Or that which furious failing
Of some high perdition
All the vain abyss spread wide

In the so white hair trailing
Avariciously will have drowned
A siren's childish flank.

As obscure as this poem may be, it observes convention sufficiently to permit an attempt to read it for meaning. This sonnet consists of a single sentence, the subject of which is *naufrage*. Belonging to this are certainly the verb *abolit* and perhaps *cela*, either a form of *celer*, "to hide," or the demonstrative pronoun. The *ou* offers either two objects to *abolir* (*le mât, cela*) or two activities (*abolir, celer*). In both cases, the two tercets are to be read as a dependent clause introduced by *que* with the subject *l'abîme* and the verb *aura noyé*. The entire first strophe should be linked to *naufrage* as an apposition, the link being established by the participle *tu*. Finally, the word *quel* at the beginning of the fifth verse marks the sentence as a question constructed as follows: "What wreck, stilled by the crushing cloud by a trumpet without force, abolishes the stripped mast or that which the abyss will have drowned—the siren's childish flank?" In addition to this is the inserted parenthetical sentence, an address marked by the otherwise absent punctuation. Within the parenthetical sentence, the word *écume* is delineated by commas and thereby clearly marked as the addressee.

The poem speaks to the foam but doesn't know what about. What the discourse intends to incorporate is the question that is the poem. The foam has knowledge that would answer this question but is unwilling to part with it. The foam hints at some event, but what this event might be is left to speculation. Perhaps a shipwreck, but this remains uncertain. By attempting to read a shipwreck out of the first strophe, the syntax leads us to read the second verse ("Basse de basalte et de laves") as an apposition to *naufrage*. Since the reef (*basse*) is not the shipwreck but rather the cause, the effect (*naufrage*) is used as a metonymy for the cause (*basse*). The rocks as a cause for the shipwreck remain hidden (*tu*) because they are hidden under the water's surface. Only the foam knows of their existence but is content with its own foaming (*mais y baves*). If a ship were wrecked, the cause remains uncertain. The reef is only made suspect by the foam. If *sépulcral naufrage* is assumed to be a metonymy for the basalt reef, then the completely groundless relationship between reef and shipwreck has another aspect, the invisible tombstone for what was lost in the shipwreck.

It is a reminder of what has died but is hidden and visible only insofar as the foam hints at its existence, if not at something else.

It is not only uncertain if there was a shipwreck, but what, if anything, went down with it. Perhaps it is a ship (*le mât dévêtu*), but maybe it is a siren that has drowned in the ocean. Whatever it might have been, it cannot be discovered except through the mediation of the foam. Since everything has disappeared, there is no way to determine what it was. This presents us with the central importance of the foam. It is the only given. Everything else must be gleaned through it. The foam is language. But it speaks in a way that fails to lead to any affirmative communication. In that the foam never speaks explicitly but only presents possibilities, it possesses the virtuality of ambiguous discourse. It might point to a reef that caused a shipwreck, in which a ship, but maybe a siren, was lost. All of this remains suspended in the virtual meaning of the foam and is relegated to the uncertainty from which the poem constitutes itself as a question.

This is not the only place where foam is used as a metaphor for language. In the poem *Salut,* written only slightly later, foam in a wine glass is equated with the discourse of the poem:

> Rien, cette écume, vierge vers
> A ne désigner que la coupe (Vv. 1–2)

> Nothing, this foam, virgin verse
> denoting only the cup

There is nothing that prevents us from interpreting the foam as poetic discourse in *A la nue accablante tu* (By the crushing cloud stilled), understanding the parenthetical sentence as a self-address, unless we were unwilling to accept the very far-reaching consequences of this equivalence. If the poem addresses itself as foam, then it thematizes itself as ambiguous discourse. The poem is a discourse of a particular kind. It is no longer ambiguous but has as the topic of its discourse its own ambiguity. The poem is caught in the problematic situation created whenever ambiguity is no longer just an event but a topic in and of itself. Ambiguity requires the simultaneity of meaning. If meanings are presented simultaneously, however, then they can no longer be kept apart. The determining factor for the density of ambiguous discourse also determines its vagueness. This vagueness can only be overcome by the uncovering of meanings in succession, whereby the density is diluted. If the poem is more than just ambiguous discourse but also speaks about that ambiguity, then it must deliberate on the meanings of the foam. This is indeed the case, since the poem is constituted as a deliberative explication of what the foam refers to. The alternatives of ship and siren ("Quel naufrage abolit le mât dévêtu ou cela que . . ."), vaguely alluded to by the foam, are unfurled, presenting clear possibilities. The poem's structure in its entirety is the unfurling of the fish's tail, to which its last word so aptly alludes.

Such a reading of the poem shows it to be a unification of what cannot be united. It not only has the density of ambiguity but also unfurls the multiple into an understandable sequence. Ambiguous discourse unfurls ambiguity, that is, it speaks implicitly and explicitly at the same time. What must be understood here is the simultaneity of simultaneity and succession, the concurrence of concurrence and sequence, the unification of ambiguity and explication in one single event. (Additionally, the ambiguous word *cela* reestablishes ambiguity within its own unfurling.) It should be assumed that whenever the vagueness and darkness of ambiguous texts fail to present themselves as correctable faults, this simultaneity cannot be replaced by an explicating text but becomes irreducible. Any explication is, by nature, reductive. What is gained in clarity is lost in density. When a text becomes more dense, darkness must be accepted. If Mallarmé's text combines these two opposite tendencies, we are left with the question whether or not some form of explication is possible that is not reductive and that, at the same time, retains the darkness of the text. The differentiation of simultaneous meanings within a succession can be achieved in various ways. With Mallarmé we find neither the preference of one potentiality over another nor simple tabulation. This differentiation occurs instead as a true alternative. The elements of succession are bound by the conjunction *ou*. Things confront each other in the alternative that cannot be combined because they are mutually exclusive. Their simultaneity as the either-or of the alternative is therefore precarious and demands resolution. The alternative includes the demand for a decision that excludes one or the other element. As the alternative *or* requires a decision, it expresses the fact that a decision has not been made. The compulsion to decide is only possible in indecisiveness, which itself leads to the formulation of the alternative. The *or* is the suspension of the decision by which ambiguity would be reduced. In that the possible meanings of the foam are bound together in the unfurling of the *or*, the decision has been postponed. Simultaneity is maintained as the untenable sequence within the alternative's concurrence. The alternative demonstrates the tendency towards clarity by demanding decisions. Insofar as no decision is made, the undecidability of ambiguity remains.

Mallarmé's poem unfurls the ambiguity of the discourse of which it speaks (*écume*) in such a way that it succeeds in circumventing any decision. But the undecidability of the unfurling discourse differentiates itself from ambiguous discourse in that it sways back and forth between explicitly different and enumerated possibilities, whereas the foam has the undifferentiated virtuality of implicit and vague discourse. If the alternative can provide meanings of the foam, and if it has within itself the need for decision, what then prevents a decision from being made? All criteria are lacking. To make a decision, the foam would have to surrender its knowledge and share its meaning. In view of its silence, all attempts at interpretation only result in fictitious meanings that cannot be compared with anything else and are therefore all equal. The interpretation of the foam is therefore in no way decisive but is instead groundlessly arbitrary. Many other possibilities offer themselves aside from ships or sirens. The arbitrariness of what is evoked by the explicit discourse of the poem leads at the same time to the renunciation of what is elicited in the interpretation of the foam. What does not yet exist in the undifferentiated vagueness of the foam is created in the unfurling discourse as something that no longer exists and perhaps never did. The interpretation is the story of the disappearance of what appears within it. The ship appears in order to be shipwrecked, the siren surfaces in order to drown. By renouncing explications of the foam, the poem returns to the vague ambiguity it is. In that the poem reads itself on a circular track and in doing so returns to itself through the rejection of this reading, it prevents its speaking from being forgotten, and its speaking continues to have meaning by never arriving at any meaning.

This interpretation of the poem remains disappointing. It seems now to say that ambiguity is not reducible and that its dense discourse can only be unfurled in such a way that the decision between its possible meanings remains suspended. The poem, seen as discourse explicating the foam, constitutes itself as an alternative and demonstrates undecidability. But in this way the poem is read in exactly the way in which it refuses to be read through what it expresses. Undecidability has now become the meaning to which it has been reduced. Instead of being undecided, the poem now states undecidability and loses it by being forced to do so. As a discourse on undecidability, it returns to the decidability of communication. And yet it should be read as the foam to and of which it speaks, because the undecidability of which it speaks is its own. This is not to say that any attempt at interpretation becomes untenable. The diversity of meanings in the unfurling discourse provides the impetus that causes the poem to foam.

This divergence is evident not only in the undecidability of possible meanings for the foam, ship, and siren. The word *basse* must, if the sentence is to be constructed coherently, be taken as a noun, denoting a reef hidden just under the surface. Nevertheless, the supposition that the word comes from the adjective *bas* is not off base. Not only are these the same words, but in the tenth verse we find the word *haute*, and height and depth are united in the word *basalte*. *Basse* and *haute* are the unfurling of *basalte*, just as in the greater structure of the poem, *écume* is dissected into *mât* and *sirène*. This repetition of the unfurled structure is not only a confirmation but also brings something into view not heretofore noticed. The origin of the word *basalte* does not have anything to do with height and depth. This connection is established in the confrontation with the words *haute* and *basse* and associated with them through sound. The word is not used here in its conventional meaning but according to its sound value, which in French provides the word, based on its phonetic proximity to other words, certain possibilities that are here put to good use. But if *basalte* contains the opposition of *bas* and *haut*, this by no means eliminates the conventional meaning. Basalt is confirmed as a volcanic rock by the lava that appears in the same verse. The verse "Basse de basalte et de laves" comes to represent the double meaning of words in Mallarmé's text. *Basalte* is phonetically coupled with *basse*, semantically with *laves*. The words are to be read two ways. On the one hand they fulfill their normal function of meaning, from which we would not want to free them, and on the other hand they bring new meaning to their surroundings with their phonetic relationship. The word *basalte*, in its internal opposition, stands for the word that flows high and low and is important both as something meaningful and as meaning. This contrary effectiveness of the word—away from itself and towards itself—is represented in the verse by the reversal of sounds that makes the word *basalte* a symmetrical axis from which the verse goes out in opposite directions to the phonetic association *basse* and the semantic association *laves*:

Basse de bas|alte et de laves

The normal and the poetic meanings of *basalte* are not randomly placed side by side but are meaningfully related to one another. The basaltic crystallization of the linguistic lava, uniting height and depth, gives the word the volcanic qualities it signifies. The movement from the depths to the heights is the eruption in which the furibund abyss rises. This is countered from up to down by the sinking of the ship and the drowning of the siren.

This unfurling can be seen in the text in another way, most noticeably in the word *éployé*, present not only for its conventional meaning, but also because it embodies in the letter *y* the bifurcation of the fish tail. The text of the eighth page of the *Coup de dés*, in which the fish tail of the siren appears, comes together in the letter *y*. A similar form is evident in the letter *v*, especially prevalent in *A la nue accablante tu*. The split from below is contrasted with the split from above in the inversion of the *v* to the ^ . The *accent circonflexe* (*circonflexe*: "Turned from one side to the other . . . orthographic sign in the shape of an inverted *v*" [Littré]) and the letter *v* relate to each other in the same way that both parts are related. Where they converge, a basaltlike structure is formed, such as in the word *dévêtu*, whose graphic structure represents its relationship to the word *nue*, which means not only the cloud but is also the positive expression for being unclothed, whereas *dévêtu* describes being naked in a negative way. The same suspension between up and down is visible in the verse "Tout l'abîme vain éployé," where the white hair of the foam whirls between heaven and sea as the unfurling of the abyss.

This passage is suspended in another way. The twelfth verse can be linked to either *éployé* or *noyé* as a more precise determinant. The abyss, which is inherent in the white hair, drowns the siren, but she is drowned in this hair, which, as the foam of the sea, is also the discourse of the poem itself. Indeed, in the verse "Dans le si blanc cheveu qui traîne," the siren drowns as "si . . . traîne" and even carries the crown of foam of the *accent circonflexe*, to which she is entitled as *reine*. If read this way, the verse itself, appearing as black on white, is the white hair, unless the hair is taken to swim between the lines. Then the drowned would only be accessible to those able to read between the lines. It is what the *trompe sans vertu* keeps secret, without keeping the verse secret (*sans vers tu*), because it speaks without virtuality. In contrast, reading between the lines recognizes language as black on white and experiences it more as an elemental establishment of meaning than in its given symbolic function. The poem, which makes the uncontrollable possibilities of language possible, is not only discourse that repeats what is given. It is also productive in that, according to Mallarmé, the initiative is left to the words themselves (366).

A speaking that allows language to thrive is no longer easily determined. A speaker can no longer be made responsible for what is expressed. The language speaks without his even knowing it. Nothing is expressed that might precede its being expressed or that is not given through it. Discourse is no longer the transmission of something to someone, nor is it the communication of something between two people. Discourse is no longer understandable when viewed as based on communication, and it does not gain its meaning from some purpose. What kind of discourse is this, and how can it be understood aside from what it is not? It is the discourse in which language foams, and for which the word *baver* stands in the poem.

Baver is the babbling of children and the speaking of those who have trouble sticking to the subject. In the older language, the word primarily means "to chitchat," "to speak nonsense." *Babiller* and *bavarder* are variants. The blabbermouth talks so much because he says so little. Precisely because chitchat is so meaningless, it is always found lacking. Its fault lies in the fact that it remains incomprehensible because it says nothing. Chitchat is speaking for speaking's sake. Those who have nothing to say, chitchat. Chitchat is stingy with messages. This stinginess is reflected in the French word *bavard*, just as the word *avare* is only slightly less stingy to become *bavard*. *Baver* is noncommunicative as a discourse that says too little. The foam has knowledge but speaks in such a way that it remains concealed. *Baver* generally has a negative connotation. It could very well denote the kind of hermetic, secretive style of speaking of which Mallarmé has always been accused. A journalist used these words in 1898:

> [This] poet, he composed, in all sincerity, never with the intent of mystifying his contemporaries, these extraordinary logographies which forged his fame, and whose key he carefully kept to himself. By what cerebral aberration did this scholar and finely lettered man, appreciator of our best classics, misrecognize, with his mind made up, pen in hand, one of the primordial characters of the genius of the French language—clarity? Mystery! He could even, if necessary, dis-

cern his own thoughts among the heavy darknesses in which he liked to envelop them. (*Documents Mallarmé* II, 39)

If one accepts the negative tone of *baver*, and we have nothing in the poem that speaks against this, then these sentences can be read as a paraphrase of "tu / Le sais, écume, mais y baves." The poem anticipates later criticism by ironically presenting its own discourse from the perspective of those who do not understand. Incomprehension is manifest when communications are expected where none are intended. Comprehension begins when *baver* is no longer understood as a negative thing. This revaluation requires the renunciation of instrumentality and the recognition of a discourse that does not communicate or that does so in another way. If one breaks the chains of convention, then it becomes questionable whether the foam conceals any knowledge at all. The word *naufrage* contains the first-person pronoun, so that the assignation of this knowledge becomes unsure: "you / Know, foam, but babble there." If the speaker in the poem had this knowledge, he could share it. If, however, it foams at the mouth, then it is either unimportant to know the extent of this knowledge, or it relates directly to the manner of speaking of *baver*, shared by you and me. *Baver* is the discourse of the poem, which can no longer be criticized from the viewpoint of instrumentality but should be understood in its positive aspects as the foaming of language.

The words *écume* and *baver* serve not only to characterize the poem's manner of speaking, they also belong to the same speaking they characterize. They not only point to the foam, they *are* the foam. The poem is the foaming of these two words, from which the predominant sound groups of the text can be derived. *Baves* is used several times as a rhyme but also belongs to *basse, basalte*, or to *abolit, abîme*, in which its initial sound appears in reverse, as well as to the many words with *a* and/or *v*. *Ecume* finds its echo in *échos esclaves* and *accablante*, but also in *suprême, abîme*, and the common *u* and *é* sounds. The entire poem seems to swirl out of *écume* and *baves* like foam. It shows itself to be an unfurling of a new kind. We are no longer concerned with unfurling the possibilities of the foam's meaning; instead we let the foam froth up, the language run rampant. The foaming of the language is the unfurling in the verse "Tout l'abîme vain éployé." The abyss is not only what reveals itself in the foam but also the foaming itself. The word *abîme* contains elements of *écume* and *baver*, and in the middle *î*, the foam comes to a head and sprays out language. Perhaps the song of the drowned siren rings out in this *î*, a relatively rare sound in the poem. This frothing of language has nothing to do with onomatopoeia, which always presumes a given meaning assigned to a certain sound. The linguistic foam is not representative but productive. The poem speaks not of the foam itself but of foam as an attempt to say how it occurs.

Whenever language foams, its message is endangered. The poem *A la nue accablante tu* can be construed as a sentence. It is therefore linear according to a discourse ruled by logic. But the difficulty in determining the parts of the sentence and the uncertain assignment of others points to a threatened grammar and to a force that counteracts it. Foam does not foam linearly. It sprays like fireworks. Everything is illuminated and becomes dim at the same time. The movement of foam is purposeless, eruption from a predestined and regulated scheme, volcanic eruption, not forward, but up from below, as with basalt, claiming a space wherein the relationships run helter-skelter and no longer respect convention. Words for Mallarmé are not closed entities with precise meaning, something they have become in everyday discourse. They have a depth that allows them to speak in noninstrumental ways. In this way, *accablante* contains *blanc*, *écume* plays on *écrire*, and *abolit* on *lire*. But the borders between words also become permeable: in *blanc cheveu*, the adjective is put in the feminine form *blanche*. This frothing of linguistic function cannot be forced into the structure of a coherent communication. Word bubbles are blown within the framework of the poem and create billowing constellations, reflect each other, permeate one another, and pop. What pops, breaks apart and disappears. What is to be communicated sinks in the foam of the linguistic gale, leaving language to speak alone. The superfluous arises out of the foam, frothing up from the broken crust of functional language. Where the superfluous takes over, it can no longer be controlled and becomes troublesome. The superfluous is by no means unimportant because it is not used. Its presence without being used makes it so worrisome. The useful is gotten rid of by being used up. The superfluous makes itself known because it is not used up as the scandalous presence of the useless. The foam is abysmal in its lack of foundation. The distressing and uncontrollable part of literature is its foaming, in which instrumental discourse is dissolved and dispersed, and in which language begins to unfurl its abysmal character. The linguistic play of words is unjustifiable within the structure of the poem. Since they have no justifiable foundation, they become doubtful guarantors of their own order. So too the dream that, according to one of Mallarmé's early insights, constitutes itself in its lack of referentiality as *men-songe* (*Correspondance* I, 207f.). Foam is dream, and the poem is a place of dreams wherein the norms of the waking world are set aside and normal relationships are confused. These dreamlike cross-connections, unconcerned with grammatical order, enable widely dispersed parts of the poem to be illuminated. Thus, lying and deceit (*mentir, tromper*) are conjured in *trompe, faute,* and *avarement* without being derived from their common usage or injected into a statement that could be attributable to the sentence. These allusions, uncorralled by grammatical structure, are the bubbles of foaming language. Linguistic foam is the play of words that remains irreducible and must remain within the confines of the poem because it is unjustifiable. The poem does not say nothing but foams over what it says with the superfluity of its allusions. In the play of allusions, language is superfluous and without foundation. It is no longer subsequential in its superficial bottomlessness but is a suspended outgrowth and sublimation of itself.

The foam stands for language. It characterizes the poem's manner of speaking. It is therefore a metaphor: the poem speaks in the same way that foam foams. But nothing is gained. The similarity between language and foam is not grasped at any conceptual level. The "understanding" of this metaphor assumes that the poem is experienced as something foaming. This is possible to the extent that the poem happens, since it is, in the broadest sense of the word, spoken and heard. This is to say that the metaphor represents the speaking of the poem, accessible only through its being spoken.

What happens when the poem is spoken? Not only is the poem spoken, but the poem expresses *something*. Speaking the poem is expressing *something*. This thing that is expressed is removed from the speaking. All speaking is concerned with making itself more dark and forgotten. As speaking gravitates towards what is expressed, it remains unexpressed. Nevertheless, whenever a poem is spoken, somehow speaking is present as the enablement of what is expressed. Not only is something expressed; language occurs, enabling something to be expressed in the first place. The transpiring language remains unspoken as the spoken, but it can be experienced in speaking as its enablement, as long as what is expressed is experienced linguistically and is not confused with what it stands for. The experience of expressing something attaches the experience of what was expressed as something that is expressed without having been articulated.

Does expressing something have to remain unexpressed? If it is expressed, then it is no longer expressing but something that has been expressed. The word *expressing*, which I am constantly using, means the expressing that is expressed. What I'm doing now, speaking about the act of expressing, which makes the having been expressed of expressing possible, is far removed by the very fact that I transform it into something expressed. To avoid this unavoidable demise of expressing, we would have to fulfill the seemingly contradictory requirement of expressing the expressing of something without letting it become something already expressed, or: expressing it without expressing it. This is perhaps less hopeless than it appears. If expressing something is not to become something expressed and thereby lost, then it must be replaced by another something that has been expressed that expresses the unmentioned expressing indirectly. This potential is fulfilled by metaphor. In metaphor, expressing is not expressed but meant. What is expressed is something else, fashioned in such a way that it makes what is meant but not expressed accessible. Expressing something can thereby be expressed without becoming something already expressed: when it is what is meant by what is expressed.

This accessibility of expression via what is expressed is bound to the intransferability of the metaphor. Since expressing never becomes what is expressed without forfeiting the expression that it is, what is meant by what is expressed must not become something that is expressed. The nature of the metaphor, which does not say what is meant, must be kept viable. Waiving the hardly obligatory limitation of the metaphor, it can generally be said that discourse can make expression accessible when what is meant does not coincide with what is expressed, which is to say, whenever it does not name, but speaks figuratively.

How is expressing something made accessible in figurative discourse if it is never what is expressed but only what is meant? The step from expression to meaning must be made without reducing the metaphor. The metaphor must not be translated but must take place. Expressing something cannot be made accessible as something expressed, because it would no longer be what it was. But it is only what it is in the act of expression. If the metaphor is to make expressing something accessible as its unexpressed meaning, then it can only do so by provoking the act of expression as the occurrence of the metaphor. The unsolvable metaphor produces the expression that is its meaning.

Something else must be added. It is a special kind of expression that is to be made accessible, namely the expression that is concerned with expressing itself. It is, therefore, the expression of a discourse that speaks with a reluctance to lose itself in what it expresses. We are therefore concerned with the expression of a particular manner of discourse, with an expression that is negatively defined by the fact that it cannot be reduced to the expressing of something. This becomes accessible in Mallarmé's poem as the meaning of the foam. The foam is a metaphor for the expression of the poem. But expression as what is meant by the metaphor is not made accessible by its translation but is accessible only to the extent that the metaphor produces the act of foaming discourse.

The transition from the preceding discussion of the irreducible metaphor to the metaphor of the foam in Mallarmé's poem has certain problems. It is easy to talk about the irreducibility of the metaphor as long as we are not exposed to it. Being exposed to it means: to experience its uncontrollability. The controllable metaphor would be the translatable metaphor. Any attempts to say what the foaming of language is are attempts at control: attempts at determining the expression of the poem through definition, banishing it to the safe realm of what has been expressed. If the metaphor relies on the impossibility of making expression into something expressed, it becomes untranslatable. The foam as the metaphor of expressing is not understood unless the expression of this understanding becomes itself a foaming discourse. In this way it falls prey to the metaphor that it brings forth in order to express itself.

The expression that is provoked by the metaphor as its meaning is initially the expression of the poem itself, since the poem says itself via the roundabout way of what is expressed. The poem speaks in such a way that what it expresses leads back to its being expressed as its unexpressed meaning. Isn't it possible that the metaphor triggers another expression? The metaphor is untranslatable, and what it means cannot be expressed without retreating from itself. On the other hand, the demand for translatability lies in the metaphoricity of the metaphor. All metaphors demand that their meanings be expressed. What happens—now in reference to Mallarmé's poem—when we submit to this compulsion? The foaming of expressing something is expressed as the meaning of the expressed foam. It is thereby possible to make the nature and stillness of the metaphor speak. The foaming of language can be described and understood at the level of what can be expressed. But the expression of the foaming poem does not participate. It is an expression that is lost in what it has expressed, that is, it succumbs to exactly the manner of expression from which the expressing removes itself. It may be that the discourse that expresses the foaming of the expression starts to foam itself. This means that the expressed meaning of the translated metaphor becomes a metaphor for its own unexpression becoming expressed. There is a gradual, not fundamental difference between this secondary metaphoric discourse and the primary metaphor. The meaning of the primary metaphor becomes what is expressed by the secondary metaphor. But in this problematic transformation of expressing into being expressed, as occurs in the translation of the metaphor, the secondary expression becomes the metaphor of the unexpressed secondary expression, and the primary situation is restored.

THE TREE OF DOUBT

In Mallarmé's later texts, the subject becomes more and more obscure, replaced by word games, a phonetic and orthographic ballet. The words are not restricted to their conventional use, but assume new relationships whose potential is provided by the alphabet, the origin of everything. This independence of language, which, instead of mediating, actually creates relationships, eludes the grasp of a reader who is looking for a message and in doing so rushes past the poem that exists as an expression and reexpression of itself. The dilution of the message and the undecidability of meaning is the flip side of an expression that understands itself less as making reality into language than as a realization of language. But not all of Mallarmé's texts are as marginal with regard to their message as his last poems. *L'après-midi d'un faune* (The afternoon of a faun), even in the late version of 1876, is a poem characterized by an unusual amount of action and narrative passages, something uncommon for Mallarmé. If the message is given more weight here, then this in no way excludes the play of words. It does confine this play somewhat, however, and allows instead a thematization of discourse in the poem no longer possible in the extreme texts that hardly *express* anything. *L'après-midi d'un faune* expresses the un-decidability of discourse realized in the foaming discourse of *A la nue accablante tu.* This is not to say that *L'après-midi d'un faune* can be reduced to a message, only that the discourse of this poem is more closely tied to an object and can therefore be more easily read for content.

There is already an indication that the theme of undecidability is close at hand in the title. Mallarmé had the words *favne* and *églogve* printed with a *v* instead of a *u*. This could be an allusion to Roman orthography and brings the poem more closely into the realm of mythology. More importantly, we see here a graphic realization of bifurcation, the fish tail of the unsolvable alternative. The theme of decision is also stressed in the word *églogue*, which can be read on several levels. First there is the poem over which it stands, recognizable as a pastoral. According to its etymology, it means "the chosen," a chosen piece or a collection of such. This could also be interpreted as an allusion, considering that the poem is only part of a planned work that Mallarmé never gave up. The word also radiates from the poem itself:

> arcane tel élut pour confident
> Le jonc vaste et jumeau dont sous l'azur on joue: (Vv. 42–43)

> as confidant such arcanum chose
> the great twin-reeds one plays beneath the azure:

The chosen is selected out of many and is thereby distinguished as unique. Here the unique is a double, something that requires a choice. I will show that this propagation of indecision is actually the theme of the poem. It unfurls in the discourse of the Faun, as he reflects on his relationship to two nymphs. We are not only concerned with a dual object but also with a dual relationship, bringing both the erotic and the artistic side of the Faun to the fore. The importance of duality in this poem justifies the attempt at a more precise reconstruction of these relationships.

In the opening verses, the Faun speaks of the nymphs. They are no longer present, and he wants to provide them with some sort of immortality. He is overcome by doubt:

> Aimai-je un rêve?
> Mon doute, amas de nuit ancienne, s'achève
> En maint rameau subtil, qui, demeuré les vrais
> Bois mêmes, prove, hélas! que bien seul je m'offrais
> Pour triomphe la faute idéale de roses. (Vv. 3–7)

So I loved a dream?
My doubt, a mass of ancient night, concludes
in many a subtle branch, which, since the real woods
remain, proves, alas, what I offered to myself
as triumph was the ideal lack of roses.

These verses have invited little comment, probably because, despite difficulties in certain parts, the argumentation of the whole
seems to be fairly straightforward. According to the current interpretation, the Faun wonders whether the nymphs were real or only
a dream. The proof that he only imagined the nymphs is that the
trees, under which he believes to have seen them, remain. Robert G. Cohn writes: "The most direct meaning is that the reality of
the woods—as opposed to the nonexistent nymphs (represented
perhaps only by roses which he mistook for them)—proves his
'fault' (love-act) was only an 'ideal' or unreal one, with a sort of
'specter of a rose,' as in Gautier's familiar poem" (16). Such a proof
should not be attributed to Mallarmé, even if put into a faun's
mouth. The fact that the trees are still there could prove that the
nymphs are no longer there (something not requiring proof), but
not that they were not present earlier. Their current absence does
not exclude their prior presence. That the trees, which the Faun
now sees, are real, is not only not proof but not even an indication
that the nymphs were not real. The question of reality cannot be
answered in this way, and uncertainty persists. The Faun speaks in
a way that makes it doubtful whether this uncertainty will ever be
resolved. The verb *s'achever* not only means that the doubt is
removed, but also that it is realized in the branches of its own
uncertainty. This possibility is supported by the fact that in an
earlier version, Mallarmé allows this doubt to sustain (*se prolonger*)
itself in the branches.

Even if previous argumentation falls apart, we are still left with a
proof. We are also left with a question: what is proven and how is it
proven? It is proven "que bien seul je m'offrais / Pour triomphe
la faute idéale de roses." This sentence seems to say that the Faun
feels certain that the nymphs were an illusion. This would support

the traditional interpretation. Aside from the fact that this does not disprove the reality of the nymphs, we are left with problems in understanding the later parts of the poem, where the Faun remembers his encounter with the nymphs in great detail. This casts doubt on whether everything was just made up. If this question remains unanswered, then the sentence that provides proof cannot be reduced to its answer. The Faun is not only concerned with the status of the nymphs but also with his own relationship to them. Words like *s'offrir*, *triomphe*, and *faute* relate to the emotional state of the Faun. He not only wants to know if the nymphs were real or not, but also to understand what they mean to him. His completely affective relationship to them is defined as love in the opening question, "Aimai-je un rêve?" The question whether the nymphs were dream or reality is motivated by this love and does not arise from an academic need to know. The actual presence of the nymphs only interests the Faun insofar as they mean something to him. Something is not loved just because it exists but because it becomes personally meaningful. This meaning is the basis for the Faun's relationship to the nymphs, and this relationship is not affected by the uncertainty concerning its status. The question "Aimai-je un rêve?" raises the possibility of loving a dream. The love of the Faun is therefore independent of the nymphs' reality or irreality because, in both cases, it is based on their meaning. Insofar as they have meaning, the nymphs are language, regardless of whether they are referentially real or not. Referential reality is unimportant until it begins to mean something. Even if the nymphs are real, the Faun does not love them as they are but as the image he has created. As long as this image, be it reproduction or representation, has meaning, then love has substance. It is not based on something external, something beyond control, but on the linguistic nature of the image. The opposite of this independence from the external is loneliness. The person for whom the other is what he means does not relate to the other in his otherness. He transforms the other into a language of his own, a language with which he then remains alone. Seen in this way, the Faun is lonely even in the presence of the nymphs. Whether they are present or not, it holds true that "que bien seul je m'offrais / Pour triomphe la faute idéale de roses." The word *faute* must not be interpreted as a love act (cf. Cohn, 16) (for why should this be a moral liability?), nor does it refer to the guilt of the roses, which trick the Faun into believing they are girls (Austin, 25). What can be gleaned from this passage is the deception and absence contained therein. The Faun's mistake, the reason for his loneliness, is turning his surroundings into language, thereby causing them to become unreal. This is described by a sentence from *Crise de vers* (Crisis of verse) as: "I say: a flower! and, outside the forgetting to which my voice consigns any contour, as something other than known chalices, musically rises, same idea and suave, the one absent from all bouquets" (368). As things begin to have meaning, they no longer remain what they once were. They receive their meaning from those for whom they are meaningful and who put this meaning in place of what is. This transformation of the other in language causes it to lose its otherness. It becomes a possession. Turning his surroundings into language is the cause of the Faun's loneliness. It pokes holes in the presence of his surroundings, which gives way to the notion he creates. In this "idealization," existence is replaced by language, recedes in its meaningless factuality, and is dissolved in meaning. The duality of this turning into language allows for a lasting relationship to the image, one independent of an external but sacrificing a real presence, and is represented in the verb *perpétuer*, which says what the Faun intends to do with the nymphs. It not only means perpetuation by preservation, but with *tuer* also infers the transition from presence to absence, the price for the appropriation of the other. Proven is the loss of presence in reality's acquisition of meaning.

The question is, how is this proof provided? The critics who want to prove the irreality of the nymphs point to the reality of the trees. Mauron (112), like Cohn, reads the previously quoted passage in this way: "Meanwhile, the shadow of past sleep evaporates; but the branches persist, remain 'the real woods.' Thus no more doubt. The Faun learns he was alone, alas, and that he was dreaming." But the syntactic structure of the text does not permit this reading. In the sentence "maint rameau subtil, qui, demeuré les vrais / Bois mêmes, prouve . . . ," *maint rameau subtil* is the subject of the proof, and *les vrais bois mêmes* is only an apposition. The proof is therefore not given in the real woods but comes from an insight into the special relationship between *maint rameau subtil* and *les vrais bois mêmes*. This relationship can be seen as a similarity, that is, a mixture of likeness and difference. We can assume that *maint rameau subtil* is a metaphor for doubt, represented by the branches of a tree that reach nowhere and protrude into nothingness, as a suspension between undecidable possibilities. The tree stands for what Mallarmé describes in other texts as a fish tail. In the prose poem *La gloire* (Glory), he speaks of "many a wavering idea floating away from chances as branches do" in connection with a visit to the forest of Fontainebleau, and Mallarmé calls the branches "flying arms of doubt" (289). If the tree is used as an image for doubt, it acquires meaning. It represents the Faun's uncertainty. This meaning does not depend on the factual presence of the tree but is made possible by the internal imagining of its structure. On the other hand, the real tree is unaffected by the fact that it now represents the Faun's uncertainty and remains what it was ("demeuré les vrais / Bois mêmes"). The Faun is caught up in the relationship between the real and the metaphorical tree, and insight into this relationship provides proof. The tree as such has no meaning. To the extent to which the Faun gives it meaning, it becomes language and is no longer a real tree, the meaningless object that it always was. This insight, gained with the help of the tree, into the relationship between the real object and the object that has gained meaning as metaphor is now transferred to the nymphs, providing proof of the nymphs' linguisticality regardless of their factual presence or absence. The question whether these are real or dreamed nymphs remains unanswered. The Faun is in any case alone with what they meant to him. Insofar as they have meaning, the nymphs have no extralinguistic existence but are only the Faun's language. The act of giving meaning leads to isolation. Meaning is not inherent in things but given by us. What is outside does not have meaning, and what has meaning is no longer outside. The external other disappears as it is given meaning and rescued from its exile to the availability of the known.

The tension between language and extralinguistic reality is not solved in the poem. In contrast to his counterpart, Hérodiade, the Faun refuses to recognize the disappearance of presence in connection with the turning into language. No matter how much he talks himself into solitude, he is speaking against language, which constantly takes away whatever he says. On an anecdotal level, the conflict is shown as the Faun's oscillation between art and sensuality. His art is playing the flute, and the process of turning into language is presented as the creation of the flute. This is Mallarmé's interpretation of the Syrinx myth. The nymph, transformed into reeds, becomes the material from which the Faun carves his flute, its sound driving the nymphs away:

> *"Et qu'au prélude lent où naissent les pipeaux*
> *"Ce vol de cygnes, non! de naïades se sauve*
> *"Ou plonge . . ."*
> Inerte, tout brûle dans l'heure fauve
> Sans marquer par quel art ensemble détala
> Trop d'hymen souhaité de qui cherche le *la*: (Vv. 30–34)

> *"And to the slow prelude whence the pipes*
> *are born, this flight of swans, no! of Naiades*
> *goes scampering off or dives . . ."*
> Inert, all things
> burn in the tawny hour, not noticing
> by what art together fled this too much hymen
> desired by who seeks for *la*:

The Faun's story concerns the creation of music and the disappearance of the nymphs, from which the story originates. The tone of the flute as the most extreme expression of the transformation of the nymphs coincides with their disappearance. Physical presence dissolves in artistic expression. One excludes the other. The necessary, but in the case of the Faun completely involuntary, decision between the two is indicated in the word *prélude*, which contains *élu,* echoing not only artistic calling but also the choice of art over sensuality. The irreconcilability of meaningless reality and unreal meaning appears in the text as the contrast in which the indolence of nature and art find themselves. Etymologically, *inerte* means the absence of art and is here used as a direct negation of *art* to illustrate the irreconcilability of the Faun's art and surrounding nature. Its inactivity is based on the fact that it cannot carry out the request to speak ("CONTEZ," v. 25) and remains discourseless. The Faun's story is indirect discourse put into nature's mouth and dictated without being confirmed (*sans marquer*). Nature does not speak unless it is transformed into language, in which case it ceases to be what it was. This is what the Faun's art accomplishes. It makes reality, which it transforms within itself, disappear. The relationship between *inerte* and *art* corresponds to that between the meaningless reality of the tree (*les vrais bois mêmes*) and the meaningful, but unreal, branches of doubt. The special thing about the figure of the Faun in Mallarmé's poem is that he constantly experiences the exclusivity of presence and meaning but still tries to deny this and bring the two together. This is indicated in the expression "chercher le *la*," because *la* is not only the tone upon which music is built but also the sign for the feminine that the Faun seeks. Both together are "trop d'hymen souhaité."

And so the Faun reluctantly experiences over and over again that the linguistic appropriation of things is at the same time the loss of their real presence. What becomes meaning distances itself (as a meaningless reality) from the one for whom it has meaning. Mallarmé represents putting something into words as dissolution by using the extreme example of music. The melody, as "sonore, vaine et monotone ligne" (v. 51), contains nothing of the nymph, but is her loss and replacement by something completely different. This is why the transition from the visual image to its purely musical realization is expressed in the word *évanouir* (v. 49). This not only points to hearing (*ouïr*) but also defines the path from seeing the representative image to hearing the self-referential sonority by the *vanus* it contains as an emptying. This strong accentuation of emptiness, created by the Faun with language and music, only shows one side of his speaking. This expression does not come from wanting everything to disappear but is supposed to make present what has been lost. This is evident not only in the initial formulation of the intent as *perpétuer* but also in the decision to renounce music and rely only on words that can assume a representative function. This use of language to "paint" something is what the Faun employs in the second half of the poem to counter its destructive effect. Language should re-present that which, by becoming language, has lost its presence.

But before these evocative discourses can be traced, the process of becoming language must be defined more clearly. The sentence where the nymphs become language can and must be understood in two ways. On the one hand it states that the nymphs are language to the extent that they have meaning for the Faun. On the other hand they are only language insofar as the Faun speaks of them. They are language not only because they mean something but also because they are spoken. They are what has been expressed in discourse. The relationship between the nymphs as language and speaking about the nymphs is thematic in the Faun's discourse:

> Réfléchissons . . .
> > ou si les femmes dont tu gloses
> Figurent un souhait de tes sens fabuleux! (Vv. 8–9)

> Let's think it over . . .
> > if those women you describe
> Figure a wish of your fabulous senses!

The nymphs are interpreted here as the figure for the Faun's wish. But they are not only figures for the Faun but also something about which the Faun speaks. They point to the wish of the one who speaks of them as the object of his wish. Since the Faun speaks of something which in turn speaks of him, he characterizes his activity as glossing, that is, as an expression that refers to another in an elucidating manner.

The duality of the nymphs' being language is understandable through this wish, the motif of their being expressed. The Faun's discourse is the representation of what he wishes. What is expressed, however, is not only a representation of the desired object. The object as represented refers back to the wish, itself the basis for the representation. The wish, based on what is expressed, is not directed toward possession of what is desired but initially sees it as something represented in order to become inflamed. The one who wishes depends on language. The wish is based on the absence of what is desired, something present only in the imagination of the one who wishes. Representation is the linguistic anticipation of the presence of the desired object. The linguistic structure of the wish in Mallarmé's poem illuminates two problems that determine the Faun's attitude and discourse. The first concerns the already questioned importance of what is desired. The object of desire, insofar as it has meaning for whomever wishes, a meaning gained only from this relationship, has no real correspondence but is only defined linguistically. Insofar as the desired object is not a true image of something real, it becomes a figure. The desired object is a fiction of the one who wishes and remains without extralinguistic confirmation. This brings about the second problem. Representation of the desired object does not happen for its own sake. It is a substitute for a time when the wish is fulfilled, a time that comes when the represented is present and the representation becomes unnecessary. The discourse of the one wishing is therefore always directed against itself and occurs with a view to its own dissolution. The wish cannot manage without representation, but it seeks presence. If the object of desire lacks extralinguistic correspondence, then its fulfillment is at the same time a loss. What is gained is insufficient for the representation of what is desired. The one wishing falls victim to a dilemma. On the one hand, as the one who has the wish, he can only want its fulfillment. On the other hand, since fulfillment does not provide the desired object, if only because it is no longer desired, the fulfilled wish is accompanied by the desire to keep the wish alive, maintaining the representation and lack of correspondence of the desired object. The attitude of Mallarmé's Faun is characterized by this necessary contradiction.

His discourse can be read with a view toward the wish after fulfillment and the wish after the wish.

The Faun has, against his will, experienced that things lose their reality when they become language. He then rids himself of his flute with the ironic demand that it turn back into the plant it once was and decides henceforth to rely only on language. Language is recognized and employed as potential representation. Representation is a replacement for what is in fact missing. Whether it is called *feinte* (v. 58) or *souvenir* (v. 62), the story of the Faun basically makes present what is not. The events as they are told can be related to the representational role of the story, allowing it to be understood as the allegorical representation of its own telling. The Faun remembers having found two closely entwined nymphs. He overpowers the couple, wanting to satisfy his desire, but is forced to separate them. Since he can't decide between one or the other, both escape. He finds, possesses, and loses. A distance is overcome for a time but then reestablished. This structure not only determines what is narrated but appears again in the relationship between the Faun as narrator and the narration. This can be deduced from the typography of the final version of the text, which adds a level of meaning to the earlier versions by changing the relationship between the one who is speaking and his discourse. Mallarmé had the beginning and ending of the story printed in italics and placed in quotes, whereas the middle part retains a normal typeface. From the beginning, the story is expressly represented as something remembered, and the Faun as narrator is distinct from the figure in the narration. The Faun is aware of this distinction in the cursive passages. He knows that the past is only present as something linguistically represented. The quotation marks that designate the discourse as discourse confirm the awareness of the linguisticality of what is expressed. Here the story is, like the inflated grape that has no more juice, a linguistic replacement for a suggested missing reality. But only the replacement, no longer recognized as such, can count as complete. The Faun speaks to replace what is absent, but he speaks against the language he is forced to use, because he yearns to transcend it to win back what is expressed as reality. But this is precisely the goal of his discourse. He is "avide / D'ivresse" (vv. 60–61). The word *avide* contains the emptiness from which greed is fed, whereas in *d'ivresse* this emptiness is turned around in the intoxication of fulfillment. The Faun's only intoxicant is his own discourse. His intoxication is forgetting the narrator's language. For a short time in the middle of his story, he actually believes that he is experiencing what he is expressing. This ecstasy of forgetting language is marked in that the middle section is not set off as a quotation. The transition points are especially telling. The forgetting coincides with the moment the Faun possesses the nymphs. Sobriety sets in when he separates the nymphs and they escape. Here we see a parallel between the narration and the narrator's changing frame of mind. Where distance is overcome, the narrator succumbs to the illusion that what is narrated is also real. Where the loss of the desired object occurs, the narrator regains the distance created by an awareness of the narration as something transmitted by language. The relationship between the narrated Faun and the nymphs acts as a metaphor for the relationship of the narrating Faun to the act of narrating the story.

The Faun's discourse seduces him into believing what he says. The discourse is determined by the desire to repress language, allowing the making of the present to count as the present. The fulfillment of this wish is granted in the illusion of forgetting language. But it would be one-sided to characterize the Faun's attitude to his discourse as the wish for self-deception and illusionary fulfillment. We can easily recognize the joy of fable-telling (v. 9) and invention (v. 58) while fully acknowledging language. This is also recognizable in the capitalization of "CONTEZ" (v. 25) and "SOUVENIRS" (v. 62), which stand over the Faun's narration as a mark of confessed language. The other—artistic, playful, ironic—side of the Faun manifests itself in this joy in discourse, not for the sake of some extralinguistic goal, but from the creative force of need. This too has its correspondence in the story, hardly reducible to a failed erotic adventure. If the Faun were concerned only with the satisfaction of sexual urges, then it is difficult to understand why he doesn't hold on to one of the nymphs. Nothing in the interpretation to this point explains why there are two nymphs in the story. This duality is important because it presents the Faun with a choice he is incapable of making. He loses both nymphs because he would like to satisfy himself with one without having to give up the other. If union with the one nymph is fulfillment, then the refusal to give up the other means that the Faun wants to maintain his wish even at the moment of fulfillment. But the simultaneity of wish and fulfillment is contradictory, the wish being the absence of fulfillment, and fulfillment negating the wish. By experiencing both at the same time, the Faun is suspended between wish and fulfillment. This suspension is a persistence in language different from the persistence of the one making the wish. He anticipates the fulfillment linguistically but is still intent on transforming what is only represented in the present. For the one who wishes, wishing is a condition of wanting that requires allevia- tion. This is different for the one suspended between wish and fulfillment. Wishing for the wish works against longing for fulfill- ment. Language is no longer devalued in relation to actuality but is a positive element that balances the language of fulfillment and cannot be sacrificed. It is no longer possible to distinguish between wish and fulfillment. Just as fulfillment is lacking for whomever wishes, so too is the wish lacking for whomever is satisfied. Lacking in fulfillment is need, just as abundance is lacking in the wish. Neither wish nor fulfillment can adequately capture the frame of mind of those suspended between the two. The Faun is trapped in language, because on the one hand he tries to go beyond language in order to achieve what he does not have in it and on the other hand must stay in language in order not to lose what he cannot find outside it.

If the story of the encounter of the Faun and the nymphs demonstrates his indecision between wish and fulfillment, then it becomes questionable whether the nymphs represent the Faun's wish. This assumption, which was the foundation for the preceding discussion, is based on a reading of verses 8–9, in which the uncertainty at the heart of the relationship between the nymphs and the Faun's wish went unnoticed.

> Réfléchissons . . .
>
>   ou si les femmes dont tu gloses
> Figurent un souhait de tes sens fabuleaux!

The sentence, which hypothetically represents the nymphs as a figure for the wish, is the second half of an alternative. It is therefore not an assertion but rather a possibility to be considered. The *ou si*, which introduces the sentence, shows that the Faun is torn between several explanations. His thoughts (*réfléchissons*) are supposed to make him choose. But initially there are no other possibilities. The alternative is thereby rendered undecidable, since it is presented as an inadequately formulated alternative. The nothingness, the discourseless emptiness of the white spaces, to which only the *ou* can refer, stands between the possibility mentioned in both verses. The most elementary way of understanding this alternative lies in the contrast between silence and discourse. In the Faun's situation, he can either have nothing or he can have what he says. Not only is this alternative decided by the fact that language takes place, but it is also too general to do justice to the special form of the fragment at hand. What stands opposite lack of discourse is not just language in general but a specific kind of statement. This restricts our room to find contrasts for the formulated possibility. Strictly speaking, only two opposing suppositions are possible when assuming that the women represent the wish. One would question the act of representation (*figurer*), the other would question the wish as what is represented (*souhait*). The first would contrast the real women with the women as the figure for the wish, whereas the second would accept them as representative but would change what is represented by them. This provides us with two possible reconstructions of the incomplete alternative. The question that must be answered is either: are the nymphs real or a representation of the wish? or: do the nymphs represent the wish or something else? From the fully formulated second half of the alternative, both supplements are possible. Since the first half is missing, there can be no decision between the two questions. The first undecidable alternative is the choice between two possible alternatives. Since this remains unresolved, the two conflicting alternatives are also undecidable. This means that both the question of reality and the question of meaning remain unanswered. We cannot decide if the nymphs are real or not, and we cannot decide if they stand for the wish or for something else. The meaning of the nymphs remains—like everything else—completely uncertain. But the suspension of this uncertainty is not a balance in which all movement comes to a halt. The wish as a possible meaning for the nymphs is privileged in that it is expressed as a possibility. It is therefore within our rights to pursue this possibility, even if only as a proviso to a hypothetical consideration. But the investigation of the nymph episode has shown that the wish in itself is another undecidable alternative. The nymphs may represent the wish or something else. If they represent the wish, then our uncertainty is only displaced one step. The wish goes back and forth between the wish for fulfillment and the wish for the wish, giving it the structure of an undecidable alternative.

In every situation, the Faun finds himself in the hopelessness of the undecidable. We are concerned not only with a procrastinator's inability to make a decision but also with the impossibility of allaying the doubt in which everything is suspended. The question "Aimai-je un rêve?" determines the status of what is loved as the object of this uncertainty. To the extent that we cannot determine whether this is something dreamed or real, any extralinguistic correspondence to what is linguistically present remains uncertain. This uncertainty is also important for the complex structure of the wish. Its goal, on the one hand, is the realization of what is wished for and linguistically anticipated. The hesitation linked to this realization is based on the uncertainty of its correspondence to the linguistic image. This leads to a maintenance of the wish, which in turn prevents its fulfillment. On the other hand, if this fulfillment were to occur, it could no longer be measured according to the image of what is wished for, which would disappear, and the uncertainty would remain unresolved. Uncertainty results from the fact that things receive meaning and value through language, but it remains unknown if they really are what they are understood to be, wished for, or loved as. The discourse of the Faun transpires as a continued confirmation of the impossibility of stepping out of language towards things. The language of opaque reality is the possibility of a transparent order to the world, as it appears in music as a pure system of relations. But the doubt always remains whether this order, which is a transposition (366) of the reality of things, is confirmed in this reality or remains suspended in groundless fiction. This uncertainty is perennial. It prevents the mind from providing its own construction with any foundation other than an internal harmony.

Lack of determination should not be seen as a character flaw that turns the Faun into a comical figure, but it touches the relationship of the speaker to the world in its essence. When there is speaking, it presents itself as the search for the foundation of what is expressed in reality. The speaker is left dangling between a reality that cannot be accessed without language and language that cannot be determined without reality. This is why Mallarmé's speaker is a faun, which is to say, a mixed being suspended between nonlinguistic nature and human spirituality. The Faun in Mallarmé's poem is in no way the extralinguistic being to which discourse can be traced back and in whom it is founded. He is, instead, language, and as such takes part in the uncertainty that characterizes everything linguistic. In *Les dieux antiques* (Ancient gods), Mallarmé considers the creation of the Faun in terms of the mysterious nature of the forest: "We cannot not see in the Satyrs the phenomenon of life that seems to animate the woods and make the branches of the trees dance, down to the knotty trunks that frighten travelers" (1254). The Faun is the tree, the metaphor for mankind's fear of a nature untamed. The process of the Faun's creation described here corresponds exactly to the metamorphosis of the tree that the Faun considers in his discourse. The Faun's meaning-giving act uses the tree as a metaphor for his doubt and is also the act by which the

Faun becomes the metaphor for human fear. The Faun has meaning by becoming language in the same way that everything real has meaning for the Faun. As language he stands for the relationship of a speaker to a reality that is otherwise inaccessible, just as the nymphs cannot be comprehended as an irreferential reality but only as figures for the Faun's wish. Only meaning, never the meaningful reality itself, can be given in language. "Abolished, the pretension, aesthetically an error, though it directs masterpieces, of including on thin paper anything other than for example the horror of the forest, or the spare silent thunder in the leaves; not the intrinsic and dense wood of the trees. Some bursts of intimate pride truly trumpeted awaken the architecture of the palace, the only livable one; outside of all stone, on which the pages close poorly" (365f.). The Faun is not to be left unquestioned as a real being but should be questioned with regard to his existence in language. Mallarmé's constant connection between the fabled Faun and the tree is important. In *L'après-midi d'un faune*, the tree is less frightening because of its movement than as an image of branching uncertainty. It is in this sense that we should read Mallarmé's dedicatory verse to a friend:

> Pan
> tronc qui s'achève en homme (113)

> Pan
> trunk that finishes as a man

With the tree and the word *s'achever*, we have a clear reference to the opening lines of the poem. Undecidability is shown on several levels to be the Faun's nature. Not only is he suspended between tree and human, but the human who grows out of the tree is the crown of the branching tree. This is completed (*s'achève*) in the person who branches out from nature in the uncertainty that spirituality and language bring into the world. The Faun not only doubts, he is the figure for the doubting nature of man, not knowing where he belongs. The world is foreign to the extent that it becomes meaningful and therefore important to him. The fact that the Faun is to be read as a metaphor for undecidability is confirmed by the spelling with *v*, which Mallarmé maintained in the title. Here the Faun does not speak but is written and is to be read as the speaker. Certain passages of the text itself, read from a distance, can be taken to refer to both the Faun as speaker and to that about which he speaks. If the Faun is the tree made language, then the Faun is also the metaphor constituted as his own discourse. *Mon doute* (v. 4) is then not only the doubt I have but also the doubt I am. And *fabuleux* (v. 9) does not only mean that the Faun is full of the fables he tells, but also that he is himself a fable told. This breaks through the fiction that the poem's discourse refers back to the Faun as its narrator. The poem is not only the language of the Faun, but it also expresses the Faun as language. The speaker as the last possible foundation of discourse proves to be made of language himself. In his own undecidable uncertainty, he himself becomes the metaphor for what his discourse unfurls.

DOUBT AND FICTION

Allusions, vagueness, ambiguity, and undecidability keep Mallarmé's text suspended in permanent uncertainty. The doubt that is at work is not to be misunderstood as an expression of wavering temperament. Mallarmé's letters from the 1860's, which tell of the experiences that form the foundation for his later poetics, are, on the contrary, witnesses of great determination and show a breakthrough to certainty. Doubt is connected to this certainty. Doubt belongs to certainty and is, so to speak, uncertainty based on certainty. But uncertainty can only be released from a kind of certainty that concerns the total lack of any foundation upon which certainty could be based. It is a certainty that overcomes itself. In a letter dated March 14, 1867, the removal of that foundation appears as the murder of God. Mallarmé at first formulates the result of his endeavors ("my Thought has been thought and has reached a pure Conception") and then goes on to describe the experiences connected with this.

Unfortunately, I arrived at this point through a horrible sensitivity, and it is time that I wrap it in an external indifference, which will replace my lost strength. I am, after a supreme synthesis, in this slow acquisition of strength—incapable, as you see, of amusing myself. But how much more was I, a few months ago, first in my terrible struggle with that old and mean plumage, fortunately, felled, God. But after this struggle had occurred on his bony wing, which by an agony more vigorous than I would have guessed in him, had carried me into the Shadows, I fell, victorious, madly and infinitely—until finally I saw myself again one day in my Venetian mirror, such as I had forgotten myself several months previously.

I admit, moreover, but only to you, that I still need, so great were the affronts of my triumph, to look at myself in that mirror in order to think and that if it were not in front of the table from which I write you this letter, I would again become Nothingness. This is to make you understand that I am now impersonal and no longer Stéphane whom you knew, —but an aptitude that has the spiritual Universe to see and develop in itself, across what was me. (*Correspondance* I, 241f.)

God's existence is not questioned in this text. It is contested and overcome. What does this kind of victory mean? God guarantees thought and language. He ensures truth. As such a guarantor, God is an authority outside of language, something only He can establish because He is superior to it. The victory over God is the removal of God as the extralinguistic foundation of language. To kill God is in Mallarmé's thinking to recognize Him in his being language and thereby to subordinate Him to that which He would have to establish. The supposed foundation of language is language and can only be raised to its creation by forgetting its existence as language. This existence as language is restored when Mallarmé talks about the invention of God in another letter (*Correspondance* I, 207). The invented God is nowhere else but in the language that posits Him. The fact that the guarantor of language is uncovered in His existence in language cancels any guarantee that there is some extralinguistic correspondence to what is expressed in discourse.

The referentiality of discourse is uncertain, but it is not negated. A negation would suppose that God, having been eliminated as the guarantor of certainty, could be replaced by the certainty of His absence. But this certainty becomes untenable the instant it is posited, for if the foundation of all certainty crumbles, then the certainty that there is no certainty dissolves, plagued by the uncertainty of which it is certain. The victory over God cannot lead to the negation of His existence, only to its suspension in undecidability. If God is fiction, then His negation is no less fiction. It must consciously remain such to avoid becoming a hardened and arbitrary atheistic doctrine. Claim and negation are both shaken by the elimination of the guarantee of language, and every Yes and every No stands in the shadow of As-If. The uncertainty, now unleashed, disallows all certainty but, at the same time, is incapable of negating it, because it is radical enough to be uncertain even of itself.

Nothing is safe from the uncertainty the victory over God brings with it, least of all the victor. This, according to the passage in the letter on the destruction of God, is equivalent to self-destruction. Mallarmé says that this battle took place on God's wing, which is why, having gained the upper hand, he and his victim plummeted into a bottomless pit. The fallen sees the end to this descent in the mirrored image of what he had been months before. This image is not to be understood as the reproduction of the original, but it has all the characteristics of Mallarmé's fiction. Whoever sits in front of this mirror has no ontological priority over the image that is reflected. He has lost himself in a bottomless descent and can no longer form an image of himself. It is the copy that sustains the possibility of positing the original. The original exists by virtue of the copy that represents something that would otherwise not exist. Without the mirror, says Mallarmé, "I would again become Nothingness." The representation of what does not exist is fiction. What fiction presents exists only in this representation and through it. What is presented has the status of the linguistic with uncertain referentiality. As with all things linguistic, the mirror image lacks the guarantee of correspondence. It is not devalued by this fact but gains its irreplaceability because of it. The image is not simply a repetition of what exists without it but leads to the supposition that what is represented could actually have some existence outside the image. For Mallarmé the subject can no longer be certain that it exists in a way different from that of a linguistic fiction with uncertain referentiality. It is telling that this uncertainty is linked to the experience of thought, which thinks itself, which comes as close to self-certainty as is possible: "my Thought has been thought and has reached a pure Conception." The self-thinking of thought can no longer ensure any certainty of existence. It too has lost the foundation that formed a basis of trust. There is definitely a self-certainty of self-thinking thought, but its validity is limited to fiction, which thought—perhaps—is. Whether thought reaches something beyond itself, and whether there is someone who thinks, remains suspended in uncertainty.

Mallarmé's doubt is the doubt in the referentiality of language. The temptation of wanting to make a certainty out of this uncertainty remains. If the referentiality of language were simply negated, then this negation could be set as an affirmative statement forming the basis for a doctrine of language, even though, but also because, it lays claim to what it negates by virtue of its affirmative character. If, however, referentiality remains uncertain, then no determination is possible. It is then one-sided to talk about Mallarmé's radical break with instrumental, everyday language and his complete refusal to communicate. It is also improper, however, to want to limit him to an instrumental use of language, as one does when one tries to reduce the texts to a communicable content. Mallarmé's fiction is not an invention without external correspondence but rather a discourse whose external correspondence remains uncertain.

As ambivalent as the position of language may be, we are given nothing else. This is also true for the subject, which can no longer be seen as an independent element that might be available to language but rather as something linguistically represented as a reflection of the possibly unrealizable postulate of itself. Since language cannot be referred back to something outside itself, it gains the initiative. No one writes when something is written. Language employs the writer for the creation of fiction. The writer only represents the capability of language to unfurl itself into fiction. Mallarmé knows no other place than fiction. Writing is "claiming you are fine in the place where you have to be (because, allow me to express this concern, an uncertainty remains)" (481). If fiction is the only place in which the writer can exist, it is certainly not a firm foundation. It constitutes itself in freely suspended language without the guarantee of extralinguistic support, whose postulate it represents: "a summation to the world that it matches its obsession with richly ciphered postulates, as its law, on paper blemished with so much audacity" (481). The structure of the mirror image repeats itself here, not representing a given, but presenting something as a copy and therefore as a postulate of an original. We are still uncertain if this has any correspondence outside the mirror. In its construction, fiction is suspended in the undecidability of its own status.

This uncertainty also applies to the relationship of fiction to the external. Certainty is possible within fiction. Here we have what Mallarmé called the proof. The proof is not the elimination of doubt in the referentiality of language but the self-confirmation of fiction, as can be read in the following sentence: "The book, total expansion of the letter, must draw from it, directly, a spacious mobility, through correspondences, institute a game, one knows not which, that confirms fiction" (380). Since language has no foundation outside itself, it is not subject to dependences or limitations but can unfurl itself in the free combinations of the alphabet. The possibility of variable combinations of letters is transferred to higher elements or parts of a book. These can be words, pages, or poems. They are no longer bound to the rigid chronology in the traditional idea of the book but can refer to each other in different ways. This emancipation of the book from the singularity of a fixed progression has consequences that are discerned in the key words of Mallarmé's sentence. The mobility (*mobilité*) of the book, whose elements are no longer sentenced to an unchangeable sequence but can follow each other in various orders, is given with the multiple referentiality of its parts. The temporality of the book is questioned by the possibility of several sequences. Every chosen order is a progression, but none of them is equal to a book, since all have equal value. The book can therefore only be understood as the space (*spacieux*) in which these variations come together. This sequential variety is the game (*jeu*) that confirms fiction. This confirmation does not come from the truth of fiction, since this would assume that what confirms—an extralinguistic reality—has a markedly different status from that of fiction. In this game everything is always already fiction. The different versions of the game are mutual confirmations. Fiction is confirmed as fiction. The confirmation only plays within fiction, which remains in an undecidable relationship to everything that is external to it. The following quote refers to the irremovable doubt concerning the referentiality of language: "a game, one knows not which, that confirms fiction." The "one knows not which" leaves open the question whether the game is only a game, for it could be that fiction hits upon a reality. Fiction may confirm itself within this game, but we don't know whether what is proven is referentially supported or not.

The uncertainty concerning the place of fiction as a whole is very important for the understanding of fiction itself. Were it to be disregarded, it might seem as if we have in fiction reached a place of possible certainty, where discourse could unfurl itself as a purely linguistic game, unconcerned with prescribed sequences. Mallarmé's texts are indeed readable as expansions of the letter and as self-confirming fiction. The dissolution of logical and grammatical relationships and the free rein given to language, which makes words speak outside of conventional fields of meaning, characterize a speaking that no longer expects sanction from a superior entity. The dissolution of this entity causes the uncertainty to which everything succumbs. If fiction is defined as an area in which language reigns freely without regard for anything else, then we find ourselves in danger of forgetting that everything that takes place in fiction is without foundation. We could be tempted to define fiction as a kind of alternative world, constituted according to its own rules. To avoid this illusion, the recognition of the uncertainty of fiction must be valid for everything that happens within fiction. Fiction must have within itself the tendency towards its own disassembly to the same degree that it is in danger of defining itself as reality, the reality of fiction. Fiction is what it is only by virtue of the fact that it contradicts itself. It confirms itself by refuting itself. To the extent that it destroys the conventions of everyday communications, it must in turn respect them, so as not to harden in negation. No matter which way the pendulum swings, fiction's suspension of doubt must always be restored.

If Mallarmé's poetry is fiction, then it cannot be read for a specific meaning, something it refuses to represent from the beginning. It is also not enough to point out the necessary one-sidedness of every commentary and then proceed to surrender to this very same one-sidedness. Instead, it should be possible to read these texts with a sense of their undecidability. We should try to sense how, in their constant uncertainty, they come to be something undecidable and how they maintain their insight into the doubtfulness of their own status. Insofar as the poem is concerned with the problematic situation of its own discourse, it is neither descriptive nor communicative but speaks of itself along the necessary route around as few objects as possible, a route that must be reversed as well. The following attempt to understand the sonnet *Une dentelle s'abolit* (A lace curtain is abolished) as discourse, which reflects and speaks its own uncertain referentiality, forgoes the search for anything but the poem itself. The desire to avoid any determination prevents an interpretation that would construe the poem as a completed whole. The poem's contradictory character, necessary to prevent a cover-up of the uncertainty of discourse with affirmative statements, prevents any conclusion. It is therefore unjustified for a series of equally ordered ideas, which always circle the self-referentiality of the poem, to take the place of a leveling interpretation.

> Une dentelle s'abolit
> Dans le doute du Jeu suprème
> A n'entr'ouvrir comme un blasphème
> Qu'absence éternelle de lit.
>
> Cet unanime blanc conflit
> D'une guirlande avec la mème,
> Enfui contre la vitre blème
> Flotte plus qu'il n'ensevelit.

Mais, chez qui du rêve se dore
Tristement dort une mandore
Au creux néant musicien

Telle que vers quelque fenètre
Selon nul ventre que le sien,
Filial on aurait pu naître.

A lace curtain is abolished
In the doubt of the supreme Game
Half-open like a blasphemy
Only eternal absence of a bed.

This unanimous white conflict
Of a garland with its like,
Having fled onto the pale window
Floats more than it buries.

Yet, with him who is gilded by dreams
Sorrowful a mandola sleeps
In the void musical hollow

Such that toward some pane
Along no womb but its own,
Filial one might have been born.

The first line concerns an abolished lacework. Something is posited only to be immediately negated. But what is said to disappear appears by being said and is expressed in the word *dentelle*. Not only is the lacework linguistically established, despite its negation, but the act of negation must be considered incomplete. If it were complete, nothing would remain, and neither itself nor what it includes could be named. We can talk about disappearance to the extent that it is something in progress. If it is in the act of disappearing, then it is still present, and the negativity of negation can be felt in its gradual retreat. The process of elimination occurs in the area of undecidability between Yes and No. The movement is clearly directional, but it follows on and as a reaction to the determination that precedes negation. This corrects the affirmative tendency towards determination and functions as its counter-weight. This is only possible as long as the process of negation is in progress. If it were to be completed, then the statement would congeal into a hard and fast No. The statement "s'abolir dans le doute" shows that this is not the case. Doubt is first the context in which the elimination takes place, since doubt in the determination of the lace is supposed to gain validity. It is secondly the goal toward which the movement flows. This would be contradictory if one were to view the negation as complete, since whatever is negated is not doubted. Doubt does not eliminate, it suspends. Only the negation itself is negated as a completed act in not allowing either Yes or No. Negation, because it merges with and is subordinate to doubt, can only be a never-ending act in progress. Just as negation destabilizes determination, doubt questions negation and prevents it from getting the upper hand. Although the sentence "A lace curtain is abolished in the doubt" presents itself as an affirmative statement, it undermines any attempt at determination through the sequence of its elements and is constituted as a constant questioning of its own discourse. This process begins with the linguistic positing of the lace. At the same time, however, the lace posits the language by which it is posited, since it can be read as a metaphor for writing, of which Mallarmé speaks elsewhere as "this fold of somber lace, which infinitely detains" (370). In that the poem speaks about lace, it is concerned with itself. It is itself what concerns itself, the meaning of its own expression. The two opening verses, referring to the poem, represent a self-questioning. They identify the poem's speaking as a determination eliminated in doubt. The poem enters into opposition to itself the moment it begins to speak. It constitutes itself as a questioning of itself. The self-reference of discourse takes priority over its reference to other things. Language does not appear here in contrast to what is not language, as Mallarmé indicates in the statement "man follows black on white" (370), but appears to be struggling with itself: "This unanimous white conflict / Of a garland with its like." This self-reference is conflicting because the poem is forced to fight its own positivity in order not to disavow the doubt from which it is created.

This conflict is also evident in other passages of the poem where

what is said conflicts with the act of saying it. The verse "Tristement dort une mandore" contains the word *mandore* twice. If we
were to explain this as onomatopoeia, imitating the sound of the
instrument (Noulet, 162), then we remain caught up in the kind of
mimetic concept of language that Mallarmé's texts overcome. The
discourse's point of departure is not an external reality that can be
imitated but rather language itself, the letter, whose total expansion
is the book. The wordplay points to the absence of an objective
relationship between the sound sequence *mandore* and its meaning,
since the same sounds in (*triste*)*ment dort* have a completely different meaning. On the one hand the relationship between the
word and the object it signifies is called into question, and on
the other hand the verse justifies the consonance it points out. The
repetition of the word *mandore* is not simply ornamental. It allows
us to read the verse as a metaphor of what is happening. It not only
tells us of a slumbering lute, but slumbering in *tristement dort* we
have the word *mandore*. The development of the resulting double
stratification of the verse leads to a contradiction. The verse talks
about a lute that sleeps, which can only mean that it is not being
played, just as the music, inherent within it, does not sound out.
But the sleeping of the lute is expressed in such a way that in the
words "tristement dort une mandore" the word *mandore* sounds as
something itself asleep. In that the sleeping word is awakened from
its latency and brought into our consciousness by the express
naming of the lute, the opposite of what the verse says occurs: the
word *mandore* can only be discovered as something hidden in
tristement dort by becoming the instrument that is played. The
poem is created as this playing on the instrument of language and,
at the same time, refutes itself by *being* the playing which it says is
not taking place. Here we see again that discourse refutes itself as
something in progress by what it says. The act of speaking and
what has been expressed neutralize each other. The poem speaks in
such a way that it refutes the negativity of its own statement.
Insofar as it holds up the positivity of its own discourse, it must
confront this negativity to maintain the suspension of doubt.

If the poem is to be understood not only as communication but also as actual speech, then it must be something incipient. Not only what is expressed is important, but also that the poem constitutes itself as the expression of what has been expressed. The second half of the poem is about a missed birth. In the verse "Filial on aurait pu naître," what could have been born is "one." The first question is not who this one is, but if one *exists*. If one could have been born, then the birth did not take place. But even though one was not born, one *exists* in the discourse of the poem, unborn as what could have been. Every potentiality, whether its realization is yet to come or has already been missed, is linguistic. One takes place linguistically as what could have been born. The birth would have taken place in the motherly hollow of the lute, had it been played. One becomes by playing the lute. It is true that one must already exist to be able to play, but only in play do we playingly create what is born. The lute, with which we create ourselves, brings us out as players. What we playingly create as ourselves is only possible in and through music. It is said of music that it was not created. Birth was therefore absent, but sounds, including those of language, are the instrument whose music is poetry. In poetry we are the language players who appear not as persons but as nonpersons. We are only born out of the discourse we create. We are not an element outside of discourse, superior to and users of it. We are first born as speakers. We are born out of the music we make. The poem as language act is the self-incarnation of the speaker. This kind of creative discourse deals with foregone birth and negates what it does through what it says. In that it happens and allows the speaker to come into being, it contradicts what it expresses. The poem as something that comes into being is completely incompatible with what it expresses. If what it expressed were actually true, then it could not have come into being. In this way, everything that is expressed is questioned by the fact that it is expressed, just as, on the contrary, the positivity of expression is itself questioned by what is expressed.

The ontological status of the poem, born as discourse from a foregone birth, is doubtful, not only in the questionable nature of what it expresses, but also in the positivity of its own speaking. It constitutes itself as its own annulment. This is apparent at the end of the poem, which relates to the past of its own birth. The past that is recalled by the conditional of the last verse is now the completed discourse of the poem itself. The poem states that the birth, which would have been possible, did not take place, at the same moment that its own birth is complete. Therefore, not only could what does not exist have existed, but what already is, that is, the poem itself, could not have been. The poem uses this tension in its expression by finishing within an aporetic ambiguity: *naître* is also *n'être*. The poem pays homage in this wordplay to the division into which it fell by coming into being while still speaking of foregone birth. Not only has the chance for birth been missed, but, insofar as the poem has become, so has the possibility of nonbeing. The ambiguity cannot be reduced. It states that the birth has taken place and that it has not. If, however, both statements are true at the same time, then neither is true. We are left stranded between being and nonbeing. We can therefore neither say that Mallarmé's poem is nor that it is not. It no sooner becomes than it is already past. But by dealing with its own past, it receives this past in its own discourse. It expresses itself as the missed opportunity to be and not to be.

The poem, which neither is nor is not, eliminates itself in doubt. Only in this way does it appropriately address the uncertain status of its own language. "Le doute de Jeu suprême" is now accessible in its relationship to the poem. The play is the fiction's constant referral to itself, preventing its reassurance in the claim and maintaining itself in the modulation between Yes and No. The highest form of play is what no other forms can go past. This boundary is reached not only when all of fiction's invention becomes questionable, but also when even the act of invention itself is objectified and recognized in its positivity, which can only be encountered by negation. Otherwise the act of invention would suppress its doubting itself. Not only is the referentiality of everything that is expressed in this extreme play in doubt, but even the expression of doubt is doubtful. For Mallarmé, self-reflection no longer forms the basis for certainty, which would again require a divine guarantor, but gets sucked into a doubt which is no longer methodical. Mallarmé's doubt is a doubt in language. Language, in speaking of itself, is made doubtful because it slips away from itself and at the same time posits itself as the very thing that slips away from itself. When the poem, where every possible position is playfully resolved, allows this tension to go unresolved, then it transpires as the place of doubt.

Baudelaire

Imagination and Memory

Images of the mind are reproductions. Imagination, then, is the ability to have an idea of something not present, of something that can no longer be directly experienced. The possibility of such an idea presupposes an earlier experience, and this experience is then pictured, stored, and reproduced. Imagination is recollection. There seems thus to be little difference between imagination and memory. Imagination can deliver nothing but imagination. It is itself the image of the experience, the existence of which results from a productive imagination, unifying sensual data into the whole of an idea. Considered in this way, the image does not remain a reproduction, however, but becomes productive. The question of the image's creation is more fundamental than the reproductive nature, since it can only reproduce something insofar as it can constitute itself as an image. The imagination, as something productive, can then no longer be lumped together with memory, since it no longer renders something already present but creates something new.

Seen from an artistic perspective, the transition from a reproductive to a productive imagination represents the replacement of a

61

reproductive aesthetic with the attempt to understand art as a creative act. Baudelaire's writings on painting represent such an attempt. His discourse on imagination in the *Salon* of 1859 follows a detailed rejection of photography, which has no other function than mimetic recollection, and leads to a critique of imitation. This is discussed in the context of the phrase "copiez la nature," which proceeds from an official aesthetic (Baudelaire later calls it the *realistic* or *positivistic* [*Oeuvres complètes* II, 627]) as a challenge to the artist. Baudelaire examines the demand to imitate nature in two ways. First he is concerned with the motivation for imitation, second he questions in what way the imitated subject is represented.

The question of motivation involves arguments that speak for or against the reproduction of what exists. According to Baudelaire, nothing speaks in favor of repeating what already is: "To these doctrinaire people, so satisfied with nature, an imaginative person certainly would have had the right to respond: 'I find it useless and tedious to represent what is, because nothing of what is satisfies me. Nature is ugly, and I prefer the monsters of my fantasy to positive triviality'" (II, 620). The criterion for the imitative value of what exists is the satisfaction it gives the viewer. Imitation is the activity of the satisfied. Only those who find pleasure in what is want to reproduce things the way they are. Those who are unsatisfied, on the other hand, have no reason to reproduce something full of imperfections. They are instead intent on countering imperfections with completeness. But in that everything that exists is unsatisfactory because it is imperfect, they are unable to repeat what already is and must create something new. Imagination is an asset of the unsatisfied. Dissatisfaction assumes that there is something better to replace what already is. The exercise of imagination is motivated by deficiency. This is, in the final analysis, also true of imitation, since there is little need for copying what exists if its presence alone were deemed adequate. We might find the motivation for imitation in the desire to hold on to the transitory, that is, to prevent the desire for what is anticipated in the idea. It is not satisfaction, but rather the notion of its imperilment, that causes imitation. Baudelaire's text does not concern itself with this issue because he is not concerned with the motivation of the satisfied but with the fact that the unsatisfied have no desire to imitate what already exists.

Something else is inherent in the dissatisfaction with what already exists. If the extant does not satisfy, then this supposes that it is accessible to us as the thing that it is. The phrase "I prefer the monsters of my fantasy to positive triviality" only makes sense if the monstrosity of the fantastic can be measured in terms of what is, if the accessibility of the extant is not questioned in what it is. The demand to imitate the extant is based on the assumption that what already exists is accessible as what it is.

It is precisely this assumption that is undermined by Baudelaire in the second part of his critique of imitation. "It would have been more philosophical, however, to ask these dogmatists, first whether they are really certain of the existence of external nature, or in case this question seemed too well calculated to please their caustic nature, whether they are quite certain of knowing *all nature*, all that is contained in nature" (II, 620). Of the two questions posed here, the first asks whether there can be any certainty of the existence of external nature, whereas the second questions the possibility of knowing all of nature with all that it contains. It is important to see that this passage says absolutely nothing about the status of nature but only undermines the certainty that the embattled doctrines of the beautiful have with regard to this status. The question, whether external nature is real or imagined, is undecided. But its irresolution is the important thing. For those who use the phrase "copiez la nature," the status of nature remains unproblematic; it is inherent as what it is. If this objective character of nature is questioned, then it becomes impossible to decouple it from its relationship to the observer or copier. The consideration of this relationship leads to the collapse of the naive concept of imitation exposed by Baudelaire's text. Whoever looks at nature as an object to be imitated forgets that he is himself a part of that nature. The artist is not outside of but in nature, and in him nature confronts itself. With this the second part of the quoted passage becomes accessible: "whether they are quite certain of knowing *all nature*, all

that is contained in nature." Any knowledge of nature that claims
to possess nature as an object is incomplete to the extent that it fails
to consider the observer as a part of nature. Whoever believes that
he is in possession of all of nature falls victim to an illusion insofar
as he forgets his own existence in and his own relationship to
nature. Nature cannot be thought of as an object distinct from the
subject. The subject and its relationship to the object is itself a part
of nature.

We should ask ourselves how Baudelaire's discussion of nature's
imitation can be understood after he dismantles the naive concept
of imitation. The conclusion of the first part devotes itself to this
question, presenting Baudelaire's own interpretation of the criticized doctrine.

> The artist, the true artist, the true poet, must paint only in accordance
> with what he sees and what he feels. He must be faithful in a *real* way
> to his own nature. He must avoid, like death itself, borrowing the eyes
> and feelings of another man, however great that man may be; for in
> that case the productions he would give us would be, so far as he is
> concerned, lies and not *realities*. (II, 620)

Accordingly, the artist does not paint what is, but what he sees. His
object is not only what is seen but also the seeing of what is seen,
that is, his own relationship to what is seen. The proponents of
imitation seek out the objectivity of the object, which is supposed
to exist in a state free from the traces of the seeing eye. A later
passage formulates this doctrine as follows: " 'I want to represent
things as they are, or rather as they would be, supposing I did not
exist.' The universe without man" (II, 627). Baudelaire counters
this with the statement that the imitation of nature can only be
accomplished by rendering one's own relationship to nature. My
way of seeing what is seen is my nature, and a work of art must be
made accordingly. It should also be noted that my relationship to
nature is the only certainty—Baudelaire calls it reality (*réalité*)—
left. Whatever the disposition of what I am seeing may be, my own
seeing is not questioned. Reality is not what I see, but my seeing.
Since what is seen only exists as it is for me because I see, it cannot

be separated from its being seen. It can only be understood as something seen and as dependent on the seeing entity. If we can only have certainty vis-à-vis what we see but not what is, then it remains open whether we see what is as it is. If we believe to see a thing as it is, this usually only means that we do not see it with our own eyes but within a tradition or as the majority has determined it to be. Everything we encounter is already in some way predetermined, and the abandonment of our own determination is the acceptance of the previously determined. Baudelaire says: "borrowing the eyes and feelings of another man." The imitation of nature in the doctrine which Baudelaire disputes is nothing more than this kind of seeing with others' eyes. We do not copy nature as it is but instead as a predetermined conventional image. The imaginative painter does not paint what others see, but what he himself sees. He is distinguished in that he remains true to his own vision. This presupposes understanding that access to a reality independent of its own being seen is a false pretense. The artist is not supposed to render something that exists outside of him as it is but as he sees it.

How is this critique of imitation connected to imagination? We must assume that the critique addresses the predetermination of the predetermined. In the phrase "copiez la nature," nature is assumed to be a predetermined original, whose likeness is to be created. Baudelaire's critique undermines this assumption. If nature is not rendered as it is but as what we see, then it is not predetermined. It does not constitute itself as predetermined until it is seen. Since what is seen is dependent on seeing, it can no longer be understood as something that precedes it. The relationship between original and likeness, as every imitation must be defined, is therefore threatened. The original does not have priority, nor is the likeness secondary to the original. The original is dependent on the likeness, because it can only exist as its likeness. If the original is no longer predetermined, then it can no longer be imitated but must be imagined. Imagination is creative because it creates an image without the predetermination of the original. The problem of imagination must therefore be put in the following terms: how is an image created without being a likeness of the original? As soon as imagination creates something not previously extant, the predetermination of the original becomes indefensible. Every theory of creative imagination conflicts with the theory of imitation. Since Baudelaire's text introduces imagination in connection with imitation, we are faced with the question of how this conflict is decided.

LIKENESSES WITHOUT ORIGINALS

It can be demonstrated that Baudelaire's texts, which seem on the surface to remain true to an aesthetic of imitation, always transition to a concept of image that is irreconcilable with the usual relationship between original and likeness. I would like to show Baudelaire's refutation of the mimetic model using three examples from the *Salon* of 1859. The first text is concerned with the relationship of the painter to nature. Baudelaire refers to conversations he had with Delacroix, who was wont to say, "Nature is only a dictionary." This sentence from the painter Baudelaire most admired and quoted on several occasions is discussed in the following text:

> To properly understand the full meaning implied in this statement, one should keep in mind the many ordinary uses of the dictionary. In it one seeks the meaning of words, the genealogy of words, the etymology of words; in short, one extracts from it all the elements that compose a sentence and a narrative. But no one has ever considered the dictionary as a composition in the poetic sense of the word. Painters who obey their imagination seek in the dictionary the elements which suit their conception; yet, in adapting these elements with a certain art, they give them an altogether new physiognomy. Those who lack imagination copy the dictionary. The result is a very great fault, the fault of banality. (II, 624f.)

We are concerned here with the effect of imagination. Three things seem to play a role: the dictionary (*dictionnaire*), the concept (*conception*), and the composition (*composition*). The dictionary seems to provide material. It contains elements that are then arranged in the composition in some sort of order. In another passage, Baudelaire speaks instead of a dictionary of "a storehouse of images and signs" (II, 627). The sequence of events seems to be that the artist first has a concept of his work and, with the help of material given him by the dictionary, realizes his concept, that is, creates a composition. This would then be the way to interpret the passage "Painters who obey their imagination seek in the dictionary the elements which suit their conception." But this linear sequence, emphasized by the text, is not unproblematic as soon as one is willing to more closely examine the elements involved. In the just-quoted passage, it is worth noting that the painters seek out the needed elements in "their" dictionary ("dans *leur* dictionnaire"). This could mean that nature is the dictionary of painters, but it could also mean that every painter has his own dictionary. How can this be reconciled with the fact that we are always talking about nature? The question, then, of what a dictionary is, is unavoidable. The dictionary makes it impossible to speak of an unordered pile of material as the artist's starting point. The dictionary represents order, not because it lists words alphabetically, but because the words it lists are the words of a particular language and have meaning only within the order of this language. The dictionary represents the language we speak. But language is not something that exists to be used at will. It is never present outside of individual speech. The meanings of words can only be determined by their usage, provided that a certain consensus exists between them. There is neither language without individual speech, nor is there speech without language. The interaction between the two is important for an understanding of the dictionary metaphor. If nature is a dictionary, then its elements have meaning. But they do not have meaning in and of themselves. They are given meaning. Nature can only be a dictionary insofar as its interpretation has become set in a substantially accepted convention. Nature as a dictionary represents a conventional interpretation of nature.

In that the dictionary maintains generally accepted meanings, it promotes the tendency to misunderstand language as an available commodity. It is the misunderstanding of those who lack imagination. Their speech can only be dependent on previous speech.

"Those who lack imagination copy the dictionary." It is they who, without compunction, stay within the bounds of convention and accept the interpreted world without any need to reinterpret it. To "copy the dictionary" (II, 625) as an acceptance of existing interpretations is therefore equivalent to "borrowing the eyes and feelings of another man" (II, 620). Contrasted with this is the imaginative person, whose relationship to the dictionary can now be examined with the help of another text. "The entire visible universe is but a storehouse of images and signs to which the imagination will give a relative place and value; it is a kind of fodder that the imagination must digest and transform" (II, 627). At first, this sentence seems to offer nothing new to the passage quoted above. Conspicuous are the metaphors related to two distinct areas. The first part of the sentence invokes the image of a set of building blocks containing elements from which an ordered whole can be constructed. This construction-set metaphor is contrasted in the second half of the sentence with the digestion metaphor. Baudelaire made use of this metaphor in relationship to the dictionary in other places, such as his essay on Victor Hugo: "I do not know in what world Victor Hugo has previously consumed the dictionary of the language that he was called upon to speak; but I see that the French lexicon, coming from his mouth, has become a world, a colored universe, melodious and moving" (II, 133). The difference between the metaphors is important. With the construction set, everything stays in the realm of the mechanical. The building blocks are present and remain what they are even when used in different combinations. In contrast, digestion is a transformation (*transformer*). What is digested is no longer what it was but something new. The elements are not only arranged in a new way, they are changed. These two ideas seem to contradict each other. Still, the understanding of Baudelaire's text is dependent on seeing both together, since both metaphors obviously represent the same thing. If we make this assumption, then we arrive at the necessary conclusion that the ordering of elements is also the transformation of elements. Transformative digestion is based on ordering. The building blocks, with which the construction is built, do not always remain what they are but change according to their relationship to other things. The element becomes what it is through these relationships. One such element is the word. It does not have meaning independent of its relationships, and its meanings change with these relationships. Ordering words means changing them.

From these considerations comes what we can call the imaginative use of words, when a speech cannot be reduced to a dictionary's convention. What Baudelaire calls "copier le dictionnaire" is the speech of those who have no imagination. The imaginatively employed word is, on the other hand, one that is, strictly speaking, not in the dictionary. Every imaginative speech goes beyond convention and requires that the dictionary be corrected. Where imagination begins, words stop being predetermined elements. This is not to say that the one speaking (or painting) stops using these elements, but it does mean that, in his composition, they are not what they were determined to be in the conventional order. Elements only become what they are by virtue of the order in which they stand. They are not predetermined and later given order but infer this order as the thing that gives them meaning.

Imagination questions the idea of the dictionary as something predetermined. The composition of the artist is not simply put together from existing material. The material from which it is made comes into being with the composition. What was previously present is not as it is now. The creativity of the imagination does not encompass the being of things but their meaning. It does not create things but meanings. Its creation is interpretation. It has been demonstrated here that the creativity of imagination always emerges when the predetermination of something seemingly predetermined is overcome. The reception of conventional meanings ("copier le dictionnaire"), understood as imitation, is contrasted with interpretation as an act that gives meaning. Interpretation occurs as an ordering, and meaning is given through order. But how and by what is order given? As a work of art or as a composition, the result of the creative process seems only to be present at the end. But it cannot come into being without somehow being anticipated, even if only as the idea of a goal towards which the movement is directed. The anticipation of order in the mind is its predetermination. The word *conception* is used in Baudelaire's text as the predetermination of order. It seems that the mimetic model, believed to have been overcome, is introduced again with a predetermined order. The original is no longer external nature but an internal concept. This does not change the fact that the picture being painted is the likeness of an original determined in the concept. We might argue that imagination is already at work in the concept's predetermined order, but this only sets the entire problem back to where it would have to be examined anew.

Instead we can examine the nature of order's predetermination in the concept. It is said of painters who follow their imagination that they look for those elements in the dictionary of nature that fit their concept. The creation of a picture is accordingly the concept's realization in a composition, given the aid of the elements of the dictionary. To find the elements that fit the concept, their order must already be present in that concept. It has been shown that the elements only become what they are through their determined order. If the elements of this order are undetermined, then the order cannot be determined. An architect cannot design a house if he doesn't know what building materials are available. The concept is the anticipation of the order. What does not yet exist is already present in its anticipation. But how can something that does not yet exist already be determined? We could surmise: as an image. But what kind of image is it that is the image of something that does not yet exist? It can't be the likeness of an original, because this does not exist. But it can also not be the original, because it would then be the same thing. The assumption that what is anticipated in the anticipation is present as an image is therefore untenable. The difficulty lies in the fact that what is anticipated would have to already be present to be represented, and that the representation is no longer an anticipation as soon as it becomes possible. This difficulty can only be resolved if we stop looking for what is anticipated in the anticipation as something rendered. Something anticipated is present neither as itself nor as an image but rather as something absent. What does not yet exist can neither be present or represented but is inherent in the anticipation as something that does not yet exist, that is, as absence. Order in the concept is therefore not anticipated as itself but as the lack of order. It would be wrong to want to understand the concept as the anticipation of order and the composition as the mimetic imitation of this internal image. The concept is first of all nothing more than the empty idea of an absent order. The order inherent as absence characterizes the dissatisfaction in light of the given, which Baudelaire attributes to the imaginative person. Satisfaction is inherent to the unsatisfied as absence. The concept as an empty idea of a missing connection does not have the status of an original. A composition as the realization of this absent order cannot be thought of as the imitation of the determined in the concept. The sequence of conception and composition in the sense of a mimetic model is thus dissolved. A composition cannot be built on the predetermined. It is a creative, not an imitative, process. This implies that imagination does not create an image as the painter's original that is then copied. Rather, imagination determines the compositorial act itself to be a creative act.

The compositorial act is not the imitation of nature, even though it results in a picture. This picture is a picture of something, but this something is not a copied original of the picture. A picture is the likeness of an absent original. This is the starting point for an understanding of the compositorial process. This is the self-constitution of the original as something that is copied in the compositorial process. Composition is not the copying of an inherent original but the creation of the original as a likeness. This clarifies the relationship of the concept to the composition. The concept is at first nothing more than an empty idea of order that does not yet exist. The process of composition is the gradual realization of this empty idea. The concept as something realized is therefore not inherent but is created in the completion of the composition. With this, everything that could have preceded the act of the creation of the image is dismantled. What remains as inherent is only the absence of order, that is, the absence of what must be created as the composition. The fact that nothing else precedes the completion of the composition results in the increased importance of this completion, that is, in the act of execution (*exécution*), as opposed to the role it is granted in a mimetic concept of art. With the imitation of something already present, the act of execution becomes instrumental, since it occurs in relationship to matter created outside and independent of it. In contrast, the nonimitative composition in Baudelaire's sense has a creative character, because it creates its own original of which it is the likeness. For Baudelaire, everything is shifted to the activity of painting (speaking). Painting is imagining.

All passages in Baudelaire's text that have to do with execution can be read from this perspective, even if they seem to be subordinate to a mimetic model. This is true of the following text from the chapter "Le gouvernement de l'imagination" (The government of imagination).

> A good painting, faithful and equal to the dream that conceived it, must be produced like a world. Just as creation, as we view it, is the result of several creations whose preceding ones are always completed by the next, so a harmoniously conducted painting consists in a series of superposed paintings, each new layer lending more reality to the dream and raising it one degree closer to perfection. On the contrary, I remember seeing in the studios of Paul Delaroche and Horace Vernet huge paintings, not sketched out, but begun, that is, absolutely finished in certain parts, while others were not yet even marked except by a black or white outline. One might compare this type of work to purely manual labor which must cover a certain quantity of space in a determined time, or to a long route divided into a large number of stages. When a stage is finished, it no longer has to be done, and when the whole route is traveled, the artist is freed from his painting. (II, 626)

What in other places is called concept appears here as dream (*rêve*). Emphasized is the relationship between dream and image (*tableau*), whereby we are to understand image as composition. We are dealing with the relationship between concept and composition with a view towards the creation of the image. When we read: "A good painting, faithful and equal to the dream that conceived it," then the dream seems to be the intrinsic essence to which the image must liken itself as faithfully as possible.

The image is not related to the dream in only a mimetic way but also genetically. The dream creates the image. The image comes out of the dream. This brings to mind our earlier understanding of the concept. The dream creates the image so that the absence of the image in the dream can be rectified. This is confirmed by the later passage on the realization of the dream. Baudelaire speaks of the creation of the image by overlapping several layers. Of these, he says, "each new layer lending more reality to the dream and raising it one degree closer to perfection." Here we are tempted at first to understand the image as the imitative visualization of the intrinsic as an internal dream image. But the sentence is ambiguous. It not only says that the image realizes something inherent in a dream, but also that the dream only becomes real in the creation of the dream's image. It constitutes itself in the image that is created as its own intrinsic essence. The dream is created with the image both as what the image refers to and as what it was created from.

But how can an image be created if it must first create the very thing from which it was created? With the elimination of the original/likeness relationship, the accustomed sequence of steps in the creation of an image has become impossible. The creation of the composition must now be thought of as a process that aims towards its own precedent, faced with the impossible task of enabling itself. The image must always already exist in order to be created, but still it must be created in order to exist. We must examine an image's creation, as described in Baudelaire's text, in connection with this paradox. The picture is created in such a way that a series of images overlap. This method of composition, advocated by Baudelaire, is contrasted with another method in which the painter begins to paint a canvas in a corner and proceeds to the next spot only when the first is completed. Baudelaire calls this process a beginning (*tableau commencé*), whereas the process of the imaginative painter is called drafting (*tableau ébauché*). The metaphor that illustrates beginning and drafting connects the two methods of painting with the original/likeness problem. Beginning is proceeding along a linear path in which each step enables another: "When a stage is finished, it no longer has to be done." The picture is created according to the building-block principle by a simple assembly of elements. The image that is created in this fashion can only be a unified whole if the order, which it is, is determined from the beginning, that is, if the relationship between the parts is predetermined and the execution is nothing more than the repetition of the extant. This is completely different with drafting. Each of the many images that overlap is somehow already the whole, even though the whole is only created by overlapping the different layers. There is no simple assembly of parts and no linear progress. Every step is not only a step towards the whole but is also already the whole itself. No order is predetermined, and yet the order is given from the start as a network of relationships that becomes ever more refined and precise. The image is not created as a sequence of elements but by the gradual division and filling of a space. The individual and the whole are simultaneous. The individual only exists as a part of the whole, and the whole is inherent as the relationship of its parts. The smallest detail is inaccessible without the whole, of which it is a part, and yet the whole is only achieved by a combination of its parts.

I will try to examine the relationship between concept and composition, made more complicated by the rejection of the mimetic model and the resulting elimination of the simple succession of original and likeness, in another part of the text. One could object that the preceding discussion is based on an overinterpretation of the text, and that it is by no means certain that the ambiguity of the passage that speaks of the dream's realization is intentional. This might be countered with the observation that this ambiguity is independent of any intention beyond the text and is therefore to be taken seriously, even if only as a reminder that texts say more than they want to say. In the preceding case, however, it seems possible to go further and to show that Baudelaire is by no means a stranger to playing with several meanings. This conclusion is supported by the following text:

In a similar method, which is essentially logical, all the personages, their relative arrangement, the landscape or the interior which serves as their background or horizon, their clothes, everything finally must serve to illuminate the generative idea and continue to bear its original color, its livery so to speak. Just as a dream is placed in an atmosphere appropriate to it, a composition, once it has become a composition, needs to move in a colored atmosphere that is particular to it. There is evidently a particular tone attributed to a certain part of a painting that becomes a key and governs the others. Everyone knows that yellow, orange, red inspire and represent ideas of joy, wealth, glory, and love; but there are millions of yellow or red atmospheres, and all the other colors logically will be affected and in proportionate measure by the dominant atmosphere. (II, 625)

The first sentence of this passage deals with a relationship similar to that between concept and composition. Everything that is part of the image serves to illuminate the idea that created the image in the first place: "everything . . . must serve to illuminate the generative idea." *Everything* here is equivalent to the composition; *the generative idea* is the concept. We might want to assume some sequence. The idea would then be the inherent, the creative. But the idea is apparently not independent of the thing from which it is created. The image created through the idea must illuminate the idea it has engendered, that is, make it visible. This does not make a great deal of difference, since something made visible still needs something that makes it visible. It appears to be something that is thought, something already inherent prior to its visualization. But then the relationship between image and idea is described differently: "everything . . . must . . . continue to bear its original color [= of the idea], its livery so to speak." "Porter la couleur" is a set phrase. By wearing someone's colors, one shows that one serves that person. This is true of the knight who wears his lady's colors and of the lackey's clothing, for which the French *couleur* is used metonymically. If the color of the idea carries everything, then this is to be read as a metaphor for *servir*: everything must belong to the idea in that it contributes to its illumination. But the connection makes it probable that Baudelaire is not using color only metaphorically.

This entire passage is concerned expressly with color and the relationship of colors to each other. What unifies the many colors in an image is called atmosphere or *milieu coloré*. This is created out of a dominant color tone, which, from a part of the picture, influences the whole. It seems legitimate to take the "original color" (*couleur originelle*) literally. Read this way, a color is no longer a sign that refers to an idea. The idea is from the beginning a color idea. This is reminiscent of what Baudelaire expresses in another part of the text in reference to Delacroix: "It seems that this color, if I may be pardoned these subterfuges of language to express my quite delicate ideas, thinks by itself, independent of the objects it clothes" (II, 595). If the idea is color, then it is no longer inherent but is transferred to the immediacy of the painter's activity. This activity makes the idea visible using atmosphere. The atmosphere is formed as the referentiality of everything to the idea. The atmosphere is impossible without the idea, and the idea is never inherent as anything but atmosphere. The atmosphere is composition under the aspect of color. The self-creation of the idea unifies the whole in its creation and postulates this as its foundation with reference to the idea created along with it. The idea is the subsequent inherent element. It is only inherent in the image, but the image presents it by referring both to it and to that from which it was created. The idea constitutes itself in the composition as the reference to its own inherence.

This clears up the ambiguity of the sentence, according to which an idea's color conveys everything in the picture. It holds true that color refers to the idea. But it is also true that the idea is color. If it were true that color only *refers* to the idea, then the idea would be independent of color, and color would only be the means to make it appear. If it were true that the idea *is* color, then the distinction between the two, and therefore the image as image, would be untenable, because the image cannot be what it shows. If, however, both are true, then the image is not what it shows but instead shows what it is. The image that refers to an idea and is at the same time that idea refers to what it already is. It does so not by claiming to be the idea, because this reduces the ambiguity, but by showing itself to refer to the idea it is. But what, then, is the image? To the extent that it is a reference to the idea, it is more than the idea. To the extent, however, that it is the idea, it is more than the reference to it. It is therefore the nature of the image not to be able to be what it is, because it is always at the same time something else.

The image that simultaneously is and is not what it is, is the image being created. The image is the activity of its own creation. As the likeness of an original, the image is a fixed presence and likewise something determined as the predetermined thing it reproduces. If the image were no longer a likeness, then it could also no longer be understood as an object. It cannot simply be taken to be inherent but presents itself as the self-creation of the image. The elimination of the sequence of original and likeness focuses attention on the activity of image creation as the nature of the image itself. Baudelaire's interest in the creative process of an image is not the anecdotal curiosity of those who look over the shoulders of giants but is based on the understanding of the image as a creation of itself. This implies that the "finished" image, insofar as it is not simply understood as the likeness of an original, must be seen as the image of its own creation. The image is the image of its own creation. The creation of the image as what the image shows is the self-constitution of the original as likeness.

CREATION OF THE IMAGE

Baudelaire deals with the creation of the image in detail in his chapter "L'art mnémonique" (Mnemonic art) in *Le peintre de la vie moderne* (The painter of modern life). This title is surprising because memory, which seems to be contrasted with productive imagination as a reproductive force, is given some degree of importance. On the surface, the text seems to present itself as a reversion to an imitative theory, as Baudelaire says of Constantin Guys: "He draws from memory and not from the model" (II, 698), and generally: "As a matter of fact, all good and true draftsmen draw from the image written in their brain and not from nature." This forces us to examine the function of memory and its relationship to imagination more closely.

The conflict is between drawing from memory and drawing from a model—the remembered image (*image écrite dans le cerveau*) and nature (*nature*). This relationship gives us some indication of the function of memory: the image the artist maintains in his memory is not the exact reproduction of the object. If simple repetition were the main concern, then it would make little sense to prefer drawing from memory to drawing from a model. What is observed is therefore not only stored in memory but also altered. We should ask ourselves what kind of change we are dealing with. The text provides clues, especially where it is argued that the memory's image is preferable to the extant object:

> When a true artist has come to the point of the final execution of his work, the model would be more of a *burden* than a help to him. It even happens that men such as Daumier and Monsieur G. [Constantin Guys], for long accustomed to exercising their memory and storing it with images, find that the physical presence of the model and its multiplicity of details disconcerts and as it were paralyzes their principal faculty. (II, 698)

Most disconcerting about the model is the variety of details. This variety is the distinction between the present and the remembered model. In the transition from one to the other, a reduction to the essential occurs, a valuation of the elements and a discarding of those that are unnecessary for the preservation of the whole. Baudelaire speaks of the painters, "whose gaze is synthetic and abbreviating" (II, 698), and he calls their accomplishment "this *legendary* translation of external life" (II, 698). The legendary contains what is most important. Baudelaire formulated his understanding of legends with the help of Victor Hugo's *La légende des siècles* (The legend of the centuries). He acknowledges that Hugo only borrowed from history what history could legitimately give to poetry: "I mean legend, myth, fable, which are like concentrations of national life, like deep reservoirs where the blood and tears of peoples sleep" (II, 140). Legends generalize, abbreviate, or concentrate life. In that they extract the general out of the individual, they take on an exemplary character. Baudelaire is completely willing to see the legendary together with simplification and stylization, something unique to certain exotic cultures, and something he calls the barbaric: "What I mean is an unavoidable, synthetic, childlike barbarousness, which is often visible in a perfected art (Mexican, Egyptian, Ninevan), and which comes from a need to see things broadly, to consider them above all in their total effect" (II, 697). All of these passages give some indication of the changes that take place in the transition from the present model to the image of memory: sketching, simplifying, generalizing, emphasizing the whole versus the individual. If an artist draws from memory rather than from a model, he seems to do so because his task is to divide the essential from the unessential, to glean the special from the general, to get away from the individual, and to see the whole. If this were the case, then the special and the individual would be devalued in relationship to the general and the whole. It would become the unessential and could therefore be discarded. But how can the special and the individual be unessential, if the general cannot exist without the special and the whole without the individual? Synthesizing cannot lead to an abandonment of detail. Rather, the threatened loss of the individual must be countered by a tendency to maintain it.

The painter with whom Baudelaire's text is concerned, Constantin Guys, is not a classicist fixed on the timeless and the general. As an illustrator for newspapers and a journalist in the Crimean War, he was intent on capturing reality in pictures. In this enterprise, great weight is given to the accidental, the transitory, things that seem to be without lasting value, such as fashion or the way women dress and make themselves up. But it is precisely these trivialities that are important to Baudelaire, because they constitute half of beauty, the other half of which is the eternal, the permanent. This dual aspect of beauty, which, among other things, forms the basis for its historicity, does not need to be discussed here. It is sufficient to state that the artist's task consists of extracting the permanent from the fleeting and impermanent: "He makes it his business to extract from fashion whatever it contains that is poetic in the historical, to distill the eternal from the transitory" (II, 694). This means, however, that the permanent depends on the transitory. The transitory is not important in and of itself, but only because the permanent is given in and through it. The eternal is not an inherent thing to be recalled at any time, rather it must always be acquired as what shines through as the temporal. The permanent must be captured *in* the fleeting. The fleeting, the individual, the specific must be captured. It is therefore not enough to speak of the simplification of the object, of the translation of life into legend. We are left with the view that the sketchy overview might exist at the expense of the individual that makes it possible in the first place. The tendency towards the general and the whole is therefore countered by the tendency towards the specific and the individual. Both struggle with one another, and yet both are necessary. The resulting conflict is characterized in "L'art mnémonique" as follows:

> In this way a struggle is launched between the will to see all and forget nothing and the faculty of memory, which has formed the habit of a lively absorption of general color and silhouette, the arabesque of contour. An artist with a perfect sense of form but one accustomed to relying above all on his memory and his imagination will find himself at the mercy of a riot of details all clamoring for justice with the fury of a mob in love with absolute equality. All justice is trampled under foot; all harmony sacrificed and destroyed; many a trifle assumes vast proportions; many a triviality usurps the attention. The more our artist turns an impartial eye on detail, the greater is the state of anarchy. Whether he be long-sighted or short-sighted, all hierarchy and all subordination vanishes. (II, 698f.)

The ability to set an object in the realm of the legendary ("of general color and silhouette, the arabesque of contour") is contrasted with the opposing need to maintain all details ("the will to see all and forget nothing"). This opposition does not permit a decision in the sense that the one side or the other would win out. Either result would be fatal. The suppression of detail leads "in the emptiness of an abstract and indefinable beauty" (II, 695) to a generality that is empty because the tension between it and the specific no longer exists. Equally undesirable is the victory of the detail, because the whole threatens to be lost in focusing on the detail. The inclination towards detail leads to anarchy. It destroys hierarchy as the order toward which an image should strive. This dual threat can only be dealt with in that both tendencies balance each other out, and the contest remains undecided. The image is created as this contest. It is the activity of its own creation and must be accessible in the act of painting (*exécution*).

The execution of painting is burdened with the dual requirement that it achieve the whole of the order to be established and that it do justice to the specificity of the individual. The problem lies in that the detail tends to be lost in the overview of the whole, and the inclination to detail destroys the whole. To the extent that the whole is seen, the individual grows pale, and when the individual predominates, order is lost. These alternatives must be overcome by turning the either-or into a not only–but also. It is memory that accomplishes this. If I turn towards detail, I must simultaneously have the disappearing order present as something remembered, and if I look at the order of the whole, I must store the threatened details in my memory. No matter which way I turn, I need memory to keep the other. Memory prevents the one from being lost by the focus on the other, and it thereby prevents me from losing myself in the one or the other. It permits the return to what might disappear by its preservation and allows for a constant back-and-forth between detail and the whole. This back-and-forth is the creative process of the image, which is supposed to establish the simultaneity of the detail and the whole.

It is not easy to understand what is meant by *art mnémonique*. Contrary to popular belief, the simple notion that the painter paints an image according to the image of the model stored in his memory is insufficient. Rather, memory has its function within the imaginative process itself. This is accomplished in the tension between the detail and the whole. So that neither one is lost, even though both cannot be present at the same time, the missing part must be remembered. Memory prevents the connection between the whole and the detail from ever being severed.

This raises another point in Baudelaire's text, which is not comprehensible based on what has been said up to now and that should be seen together with the role of memory. Whenever speaking of the activity of painting and the importance of technical ability, it is emphasized that the execution must be carried out as quickly as possible. We should question the need for this hurry. This haste is based on the fear that what is to be captured in an image could disappear before it is captured. We should not be satisfied with thinking of certain objects as unstable and therefore only available for short periods of time, even though this may often be the case for a painter, such as Guys, trying to capture the contemporary. But even these unstable objects are remembered, and it is telling that speed is also important to the painter who paints from memory, even though the state of the object is less precarious. This haste must be explained another way, but even the differentiated way is of little help in understanding the role of memory. It has been shown that the painter is at all times in danger of losing the whole, whenever he concentrates on the detail, and the reverse is true when the detail is lost by focusing on the whole. This could explain the fact that one must be abandoned in favor of the other as soon as it is achieved. The constant fear that the detail could be lost in the whole and vice versa should encourage a constant and hasty back-and-forth between the two. It remains to be proven that such a movement really does exist. But right now we are at a loss to explain it. If memory takes over the task of making available whatever might be forgotten, then haste should be unnecessary. If, on the other hand, Baudelaire constantly seems to demand this rush, then whatever might disappear before it can be turned into an image is apparently not something that can be preserved by memory. We must therefore ask what it is that this rapid execution is supposed to save from destruction.

There are several passages that deal with haste. With the exception of *Le peintre de la vie moderne*, they all refer to Delacroix. This is already the case in the 1846 *Salon* (II, 433). The two excerpts that will be discussed come from Baudelaire's later writings. The first quote is from the *Salon* of 1859:

> If a very clean execution is necessary, that is because the language of the dream must be very cleanly translated; if it must be very rapid, it is so that nothing is lost of the extraordinary impression that accompanied the conception. (II, 625)

The second quote is from *L'oeuvre et la vie d'Eugène Delacroix* (The work and life of Eugène Delacroix):

> He once said to a young man of my acquaintance: "If you have not sufficient skill to make a sketch of a man throwing himself from a window in the time it takes him to fall from the fourth floor to the ground, you will never be capable of producing great machines." This enormous hyperbole seems to me to contain the major concern of his whole life, which was, as is well known, to achieve an execution quick and sure enough to prevent the smallest particle of the intensity of action or idea from evaporating. (II, 763f.)

Both texts explain why the execution must be quick. Both passages state that something is lost without haste. In the first case, what should be preserved is called "the extraordinary impression that accompanied the conception." In the second case, this is "the intensity of action or idea." The parallel is obvious. Not the object or its image are threatened but a certain way of experiencing the object. This is not simply a matter of perception. Instead, one's relationship to this object is emotionally charged. It is characterized by what Baudelaire calls intensity. This intensity is introduced as the thing that memory cannot preserve and that can be lost without quick painting. Apparently only the act of painting itself is able to save this intensity in the image. But we still do not understand this intensity nor its relationship to painting.

When a man jumps out of a window, how is what Baudelaire calls "the intensity of action or idea" related to the spectator? Certainly the impression of whomever witnesses such an event is related to the expected outcome. This expectation anticipates the outcome at the beginning. In the middle of the jump, the fall is already present. This presence of the whole in each moment of movement is the intensity of the experience of the fall. If I see the man at a height of three stories, then the intensity of the impression lies in knowing, at that same instant, that he has already jumped out of a window and that he will land on the ground. No single moment of the fall is witnessed in isolation; rather each part constantly refers to the whole of which it is a part. The intensity is based on the presence of the whole sequence in each of its phases. Baudelaire is no stranger to such an understanding of intensity, and it can be found again in other relationships. The intensity as just characterized appears in conditions of the mind that result from drug use but generally belongs to the realm Baudelaire calls *surnaturel*. In his diary we read: "The supernatural comprises the general color and accent, or intensity, sonority, limpidity, vibravity, depth, and reverberation in space and time" (I, 658). Radiation from a point into a breadth or depth is part of this *surnaturel*. Shortly after this passage, there is a sentence that relates exactly to the connection made here, even if it does introduce entirely new terminology: "In certain almost supernatural states of mind the depth of life is revealed in its entirety in the spectacle, as ordinary as it is, which you have before your eyes. It becomes the symbol" (I, 659). The same sentence can be found again with slight alterations in *Le poème du hachisch* (Hashish poem; I, 430). The symbol is the individual that represents the whole. The symbolism of the individual in which the whole is present determines the intensity of the frame of mind with which Baudelaire is concerned ("certain almost supernatural states of mind"). Accordingly, the intensity of the experience is determined by the fact that the experience of the individual does not stop there but goes on to a whole of which the individual is a part.

We must understand the transfer of intensity to an image in light of this definition. Although Baudelaire never seems to expressly develop this transition, our question can certainly be clearly posited from the realities of the texts. The goal is the preservation of intensity, and we may assume that this intensity can be lost, that memory is apparently not capable of preserving it, and that finally the loss of this intensity can be prevented through quick execution. This essentially anticipates the solution to our question, even though it is not yet understood. The preservation of intensity is made possible by its immediate transposition in the act of painting. Nothing besides the movement of the brush can prevent the disappearance of intensity. We must now examine this transfer of intensity in action.

Intensity is defined as the experience of the whole in the individual. Important is how the relationship between the individual and the whole is constituted in an intense experience. This is, without a doubt, a referential relationship, as the appearance of the symbol in this matter clearly shows. It is clear, however, that it is not enough to see in the individual a symbol for the whole. This symbolic relationship would be emotionally neutral, and it would be hard to understand wherein the intensity of such a relationship would lie. It would be equally difficult to fathom how such a relationship could be threatened, since the fact that one stands for the other can very easily be remembered without compromising the reference in any way. Intensity is the experience of a different kind of referential relationship than exists between a sign and its signified. To better understand this relationship, I return to the fall from the window. Each individual moment of this fall is related to and stands for the whole of the fall in my experience, not the way a sign stands for a signified, but in such a way that I experience the single moment as one that pushes past itself towards a whole. The whole is inherent in the individual that strives to complete itself by going beyond itself. Reference in this case is not a standing for something else but a striving beyond oneself. The individual is less a representative of the whole than something driving towards the whole. The intensity of this experience of the individual as something striving beyond itself is at the same time its downfall. The experience of the individual requires a completion of the movement that leads from the individual to the whole. The intensity of the experience of the individual is based on the individual's reference to the whole. But in this reference, the individual points to the whole through movement. The experience of the individual moment is therefore necessarily converted into movement and aims for the realization of the whole. It can be said that the spectator who watches the fall has already realized it in his imagination, and that the transformation of perception in the imaginative act is what is called the intensity of his experience.

This illustrates the transformation of an experience in an act, but this is by no means the same as the act of the painter who retains something in an image. What I have tried to describe is what happens to everyone, and what everyone who witnesses an event does. More happens with the painter, because the experience of the individual is not only realized in the imaginative act of the movement's whole, it also causes the movement of the brush, the act of painting. How is this done, and how does this act preserve the intensity of the experience? I ask the question based on the example that Baudelaire takes from Delacroix. We will assume that whoever sees a man jumping out of a window also draws this man, and that the intensity of the experience of this spectator is preserved in this act. The intensity of the experience consists of the fact that in each moment of the fall the whole of the fall is given, that in each moment the movement is already completed in thought. If the falling man is to be drawn, then this can only mean that such a moment is retained. Movement can only be drawn in that a particular moment is taken and presented in such a way that allows the movement to be deduced. The task of whomever draws the falling man is to fix the given situation in one isolated instant. He must not draw a sequence of moments but a concurrence of the contemporaneous, which, in the chosen instant, stand in a particular relation to each other. Primary for the drawer is no longer a sequence of events but rather a spatial construct of relationships. He is concerned with the correct position of body parts and the situation of the falling man in his surroundings. This spatial coincidence is the drawing, which can only be created through the movement of the pen. The spatial simultaneity therefore presumes a sequence. This is the result of the act of drawing. The movement of the pen is experienced in a way that is similar to the movement of the fall. It is not an event removed that is simply watched, but a guided movement. For the artist, the whole is the final order of the elements in the simultaneity of coincidence to which the movement of the pen must lead. Wherever the pen is, it strives from this single point towards the whole, because every line must be directed towards the whole. Every line contains the whole. We could call this the intensity of the act of drawing, and we would understand what is meant by the preservation of intensity if we recognize that an analogy exists between the experience of the falling man's movement and the experience of drawing with regard to intensity. We are therefore not concerned with fixing the intensity by reproducing what was experienced. Instead the intensity is transformed in the act of drawing. To understand this relationship we must accept that there is no causal connection between the intensity of the experience of falling and that of drawing. This is also true with regard to the quickness of the movement. There is no need to draw quickly just because the man to be drawn is falling quickly. The intensity of the experience of drawing excludes any delays in the drive of the individual beyond itself towards the whole. The speed of execution is based on the nature of the act of drawing itself and not on the object to be drawn.

One might argue against all that has been said by pointing out that it is based too much on the rather extraordinary example of a man who jumps out of a window and can therefore only be of rather limited value. This argument does not stand if one considers the importance given the example by the result of the investigation. It has absolutely no determining influence on the act of drawing but is used to show the movement Baudelaire calls *exécution* with the help of a movement that is analogously experienced.

How can we relate these thoughts concerning intensity and the speed of execution to what was said earlier about memory? The most important result of our examination of memory was that the task of memory was not to preserve something that had preceded a productive process, such as an original, but that it has its function within the productive process itself. This process is required to prevent what can be called the individualization of the individual, and what Baudelaire himself called anarchy in the *Salon* of 1859.

Memory assures us that we will not become lost in the details of the detail and that the connection between the individual and the whole is maintained. In that memory retains the presence of the whole, it allows the ordering of the individual. The whole is not preserved as something present in memory, since it is the very thing that is supposed to be created by the compositional act. The whole is therefore remembered as what is absent. It can only constitute itself in the ordering of the individual. Memory of the whole as something absent is therefore created by the act of ordering; in other words, it keeps us from remaining with the individual and drives the movement towards the whole. The movement of the pen rushes towards the whole, remembered in memory as something absent. This makes the desired connection accessible. Memory of the absent whole, a part of the experience of the individual, is the intensity caused by the movement of the pen as it aims beyond the individual.

THE SWAN

We might ask ourselves if the function of memory in the imaginative process, as it is presented in Baudelaire's writings on art theory, can contribute to an understanding of his poems. This seems at first unlikely, based on the verses that come most readily to mind in connection with Baudelaire and memory. In lines like "Je sais l'art d'évoquer les minutes heureuses" (I know the art of evoking happy minutes [I, 37]), or

> Charme profond, magique, dont nous grise
> Dans le présent le passé restauré! (I, 39)

> Deep charm, magical, whose restored past
> Renders us gray in the present!

memory is celebrated as an act of realization and must be understood as mimetic memory insofar as it reproduces past things the way they were. In the writings on painting, however, the topic of evocative speech is always key, and it requires a certain interpretive effort to construe the memory of something absent as the mover of imaginative movement. The question of why this link to evocative memory remains is not easy to answer. Leaving this aside for a moment, we can investigate whether some other kind of memory is at work behind the explicit evocation in the poems. This will be discussed using the example of *Le cygne* (The swan; I, 85–87).

The poem is about a series of figures, all of whom have lost something they remember and who, in turn, are remembered by the speaker. All these figures are nostalgically bound to their past. They mourn their loss and want to recover it. This is most clearly demonstrated in the character of Andromache, taken from the third book of the *Aeneid*, who rebuilds a miniature home in exile ("I recognize a small Troy, and a simulated great Pergamus" [3, vv. 349–51]) and makes offerings at Hector's empty grave ("At the shores of a false Simoïs Andromache sacrificed to the remains" [3, vv. 302–3]). The mimetic character of evocative memory is unmistakable. The lost past is replaced by its likeness so that the illusion of its presence can be created. Baudelaire's verse "Auprès d'un tombeau vide en extase courbée" (Beside an empty tomb in bent ectasy [v. 39]) might refer to the copy being confused with the real grave, because its nature as an image is forgotten, and the boundary between original and likeness is blurred. This is also made clear by Virgil: Andromache seems confused when Aeneas suddenly appears ("Are you coming toward me, a real form, a true messenger, goddess-born?" [3, vv. 310–11]). Forgetting the past tense of the past would represent its successful and complete representation as the restoration of the lost present. All nostalgic memory has the desire to completely restore the past, even when this desire can only express itself as lament in the knowledge of its unattainability. This is true of all figures who appear in the poem, for the swan whose heart yearns for the waters of his homeland, and for the African woman who searches for the palms of her home beyond a wall of fog.

Despite all the examples of the never-ending desire for an evocative realization of the present, it would be wrong to declare the roll of memory in this poem to be self-evident. We must above all try to understand why so many cases of the same behavior are presented. The story of the swan does not add anything to the story of Andromache. It remains a complete mystery why the second half of the poem adds a list that, for the most part, simply recounts very general situations ("to whomever," "to the captives," "to the conquered"). The reason for this aggregate of examples is to be found by examining their relationships. The connection lies in the fact that all the figures are present as remembered by the speaker. "I am thinking of . . ." is the phrase that, throughout the entire poem, demonstrates the correlation between what is evoked and the remembrances of the poet. What kind of memory is this, and what kind of relationship is established between the individual episodes?

The memory of the poet also seems at first to evoke the past, and the text tells us how this process proceeds: the thought of Andromache calls to mind the image of the swan, encountered by the poet where the carousel now stands. The transition from Andromache to the swan is easy to follow, since both episodes are analogous and can therefore refer to each other metaphorically. Thanks to this similarity, the Andromache story is able to trigger the memory of the swan:

> Ce Simoïs menteur . . . ,
> A fécondé soudain ma mémoire fertile (Vv. 4–5)

> This lying Simoïs . . . ,
> Suddenly impregnated my fertile memory

The one functions as a substitute for the other and can elicit its realization. The relationship between Andromache and the swan is therefore not much different from the relationship that exists within the Andromache story between the make-believe and the real Simoïs. Andromache would be the means by which a past is made accessible through evocation. But Andromache is a memory, and it is fair to ask how it is that Baudelaire thinks of her at precisely this moment. If we are unsatisfied with anecdotal chance and don't want simply to forego an explanation, then we must assume that he thinks of Andromache while crossing the carousel. This is only clear if the place has acquired some meaning in connection with this memory. The place in its new form is experienced as having changed (*le nouveau Carrousel*). This awakens the memory of its previous condition, that is, of the old Paris (*le vieux Paris*) and of the swan that belongs in this context. The swan, as exile, reminds us of Andromache. This contradicts the just-established sequence. The consequence of this contradiction is simple but of considerable significance for the understanding of the text: the relationship between Andromache and the swan is interchangeable.

This memory is different from nostalgic memory, where such a reversal would be impossible. Troy and Epirus cannot be exchanged in Andromache's mind, because one is a lost reality and the other is only an image. These priorities are no longer valid for the speaker in *Le cygne*. He is concerned with the relationship between memories that are equal. It doesn't matter whether the memory of Virgil's text evokes the memory of the swan or whether the swan reminds us of Andromache. What does matter is the relationship between memories and the relationship between memories and the one remembering. This relationship is not nostalgic. The swan as the object of memory does not have the status of something lost, which we lament as the swan laments the lost lake. The attempt to read the poem as an elegy of old Paris does not get us very far. The reversibility of the relationship between what is remembered and the one who evokes the memory leads to a neutralization of the chronology. The nostalgic's time is irreversible and experienced as a constant losing. The past is a lost presence. This is true of all the characters who appear in the poem with the exception of the one who remembers them. He does not lament something lost but instead thinks about having lost, the situation of the others. Andromache, the swan, and their relatives all lament something they have lost and that lives on in their memories as a lost presence. The one in whom all these memories gather does not invoke a specific loss but loss as the one thing common to all. None of the situations listed can make accessible the particular kind of memory the poem represents, because any memory of loss, to the extent that it remains concentrated on the objectivity of the loss, covers up the loss as such.

We can only become conscious of loss as such if the bond to the loss is loosened. In the poem this is achieved by piling up examples of nostalgic obsession with loss. The resulting inventory of examples produces something decidedly new. The constancy of loss shines through the manifold possibilities of experiencing loss. In the grand movement of losing into which the one and then the other withdraw, loss remains constant. The constancy of the experience of loss is what Baudelaire calls melancholy:

> Paris change! mais rien dans ma mélancolie
> N'a bougé! (Vv. 29–30)

> Paris changes! yet nothing in my melancholy
> has budged!

The melancholic appears here as the opposite of the nostalgic. He is characterized not by lamenting a specific loss but by the obsession that everything must be lost. He is no longer concerned with the past but rather with passing. With this, the objects of loss become fairly arbitrary and interchangeable, of equal value, and even indifferent, simple elements of enumeration. The past is no longer lamented as a lost presence but represents through its being past the passing of what is transient. In light of this transience, each passing or past falls victim to an arbitrariness that makes the attempt to hold on seem useless. The nostalgic bond to the lost is a revolt against a transience of which the melancholic is no longer capable. He is prevented by his own indifference from clinging to this or that. He is no longer in danger of losing himself in each object, as is a nostalgic. Instead he is threatened with the complete loss of objectivity and sinks into an objectless abyss.

Objects don't disappear in Baudelaire's poem, they become allegories. The allegorization of the world is very closely linked to melancholy. It presents to the melancholic the possibility of a constructive behavior. The melancholic neither clings nostalgically to what is lost nor loses himself in emptiness but experiences the permanence of transience in the impermanence of the transient. This allegorization overcomes the nostalgic bond to objects. One might be tempted to see the loosening of this bond in *Le cygne* as present in what is remembered, since what is remembered is not arbitrary but rather a series of examples of nostalgic memory. This remembering is thereby somewhat removed and becomes itself the object of remembering. But therein lies the danger that nostalgia will remain uncontested. The person remembering can assume the attitude of his characters, whose nostalgic memories become his own, and thus fall prey to nostalgia instead of overcoming it. It is important for an understanding of Baudelaire's poem that the poet does not, or does not exclusively, identify himself with these nostalgics, the objects of his remembering. The sense of the poem would be lost if we were to take Andromache or the swan as adequate representatives of the speaker. The speaker shares in the objects of his memory to the extent that nostalgia is by no means finally defeated, but he also accomplishes a critical separation from them in that he refuses to accept the lament of loss.

Nostalgia, or falling victim to what is remembered, is overcome by enumeration. The function of this enumeration and its dominance in the second half of the poem must be questioned. The transition from one to the other creates a distance to the individual. This individual is no longer employed only by itself and lamented for its own sake but, in conjunction with the enumeration of all like things, represents a generality for which it serves as an example. The fact that things are no longer considered in their simple presence or absence but rather in their meaning is what Baudelaire calls allegorization. Everything becomes allegory: that is, nothing is exhausted in its being here, but everything has something missing within itself and therefore has meaning. What is meant is the other to which we point, that which the meaning lacks. Meaning is always a hollowing out of presence. It remains hidden as long as things are considered only in terms of current or lost presence, thus hiding their internal hollowness. This is the case with nostalgics, who only know what is present and what is lost but are unable to anticipate loss in the present. In contrast, the present always holds up its own emptiness for those who see allegorically and is experienced not as something present but as something passing. If the experience of things is always accompanied by the memory of their transience, then the possibility, if not the desire, of holding on to the transient must also be recognized as transient. The fixation on the presence of the present is avoided. Instead of clinging to the present, losing it, and becoming nostalgic, one can avoid loss by accepting the present as always passing and then leaving it. Enumeration is such a leavetaking. In the transition to the subsequent, the previous is accepted as untenable. This transience is now no longer something suffered forcibly but construed and produced in the rhythm of enumeration. Instead of suffering loss, we effect renunciation.

Memory is effective in enumeration. This memory is not mimetic and evocative, since its function is to prevent falling victim to images. Important is not the memory of the list but the need to list, the constantly repeated renunciation of what is listed. The need to enumerate exists as the danger of lingering in the individual threatens. Only those exposed to the lure of memory must be reminded of its transience. The movement of enumeration lasts as long as the danger of the individual's nostalgic stagnation prevails. As this danger is never totally overcome but is resurrected at every step of enumeration, the movement becomes never-ending and merges at the end of the poem with an undetermined continuation: "a bien d'autres encor" (to still many others). The tension between nostalgic obsession with things and allegorical escape from them does not find a solution in the sense of a resolution. It is instead what results from the movement of enumeration, its mover, and cannot be reduced by any decision. This tension is palpable in the first strophe of the poem's second part, where allegorization is starkly confronted by the material weight of memories, something understandable only in the context of a nostalgic relationship:

> tout pour moi devient allégorie,
> Et mes chers souvenirs sont plus lourds que des rocs. (Vv. 31–32)

everything for me becomes allegory,
and my precious recollections are heavier than rocks.

The same conflict between the temptation to hold on to the memory and distancing oneself from it also makes the difficult verses of the final strophe, those dealing with memory, more accessible:

Ainsi dans la forêt où mon esprit s'exile
Un vieux Souvenir sonne à plein souffle du cor! (Vv. 49–50)

Thus in the forest where my spirit takes exile
An old Memory rings in full force from the body!

It is at first difficult to see how these verses fit the list, which continues in the last two lines of the poem. We might surmise that the person remembering has placed himself in the series of his own examples. Just as all others have lost something to which they cling, so (*ainsi*) the mind of the speaker, too, reflects his loss in exile. The poet would then be included among those of whom he speaks. But the fact that he does speak makes it impossible for him to be in the same category. It is not incorrect, but certainly inadequate, to read these verses on the same level as the others. The I is not, like the other characters of the poem, only one element of a list, but the enumerator himself. What happens here affects the enumerator. What has up to now been said of exile and memory is true of him as well. The two verses must be seen as a characterization of what occurs in the poem as enumeration and must be read in this sense.

The forest represents the many memories that have been gathered in the list. In each of these memories, the mind is in danger of losing itself in the loss. To the degree that he succumbs to this danger and the fascination of the memory, he estranges himself and forces himself into exile. But this is exactly what the list should prevent. The list's task is to undo the fixation on the individual. This requires the memory's trumpet call in the forest of enumeration. This memory recalls the wandering mind to itself, reminds it of itself, as the hunter's horn calls an end to the hunt and a return home. What is forgotten in nostalgic memory under the burden of memory is here recalled to memory: the act of remembering as the possibility of an evocation based on the transience of the transient, something that must always be present to form the nostalgic bond. *Un vieux Souvenir* must be understood as the memory of the act of remembering.

This expression shows a curious internal tension. The capitalization of *Souvenir* indicates that the memory appears here as a personified allegory. A distancing from all objects of individual memories has already taken place, and remembering becomes itself the possibility of remembering what has been remembered. This is contradicted by the indefinite article, indicating that an individual memory might be meant. *Un vieux Souvenir* represents both the generality of remembering and the specificity of a single memory. Baudelaire's understanding of memory depends not on the reduction of this tension but rather on its unfolding.

An attempt at this unfolding can proceed from the fact that remembering is only accessible through individual memories. *Something* is always remembered, and the realization of this something is memory's achievement. But in looking to individual memory, remembering itself can be lost. To regain it, we must distance ourselves from what is remembered. This must occur in such a way that does not abandon memory along with what is remembered. The memory must live on but in a way that overcomes the fixation on what is remembered. This is accomplished by substituting one memory for another, that is, through enumeration. Remembering is accessible through the constant withdrawal from everything remembered or listed. This is why the memory of the act of remembering sounds out in the forest. The act of remembering can never become a remembered object, in which the memory could quiet itself. It can only appear or sound out in enumeration as a never-ending distancing from the remembered or the listed. Positively speaking, this means that each single memory becomes an allegory of that memory to the extent that each is a part of the enumeration. The nostalgic memory (Andromache, the swan) has meaning in that it is listed along with other, similar things. The remembered nostalgic memory signifies the act of remembering, which, taken as a single instance, has been forgotten. It does so when it becomes part of an enumeration. *Un vieux Souvenir* is individual memory in enumeration. But it is also the act of remembering as it is enumerated that is given meaning by individual memory. It is this that sounds out in the list (*dans la forêt*) from the single memory (*un souvenir*), and it is the general act of remembering that makes this possible.

Memory of the act of remembering is also a memory of the fact that what is remembered is something past and that remembering itself depends on transience. If the nostalgic turns memory against transience and by doing so hopes to fight off the transience of the transient, then he negates the prerequisite that makes all this possible in the first place. This is opposed by a memory that makes not only the past present. The transience of the transient reminds him, yet attempts to hold nothing, because it reminds him of his own impermanence and also makes any sojourn impermanent.

A sojourn with the remembered is rejected in enumeration, the constitution of the poem's speech. Enumeration is a means to construe the sequence of speech. What was said earlier about the creation of images, comparable to enumerating speech, intrudes into our discussion. Movement is always what is prevented by staying and resting. In the first instance, it is the intensity that drives the individual toward the missing whole, of which it is a part. Movement goes to the construct that ties sequence to simultaneity and then comes to rest. In enumeration, on the other hand, the individual is abandoned, because it is itself transient. Movement here does not go to the stability of the construct's whole, and integration of the individual is not even attempted. Enumeration as a construct is the rhythmic realization of transience and is unopposed. But the renunciation of the individual enumeration's self-satisfaction must always be kept alive with the memory of its own transience. The danger of forgetting, that is, deference to the individual, still exists where the memory of the transience of the remembered is put into words. This occurs in the image of the trumpet call in the forest, something that demands attention for its own sake and is difficult to ignore. Nevertheless the image prevents us from succumbing to it. As the image of a sound that fades away, it recalls a memory and thereby effects a disengagement from itself and maintains the movement of enumeration.

A Renunciation of Understanding

Baudelaire's prose poem *Chacun sa chimère* (To every man his chimera) tells about an encounter with several men who are carrying chimeras on their backs. They trek through a desert with this load not knowing where they are going. After the caravan disappears, the observer wonders what it all means but soon gives up his attempt to uncover their secret and sinks into apathy. Given a story not understood by the very person telling it, we must ask ourselves what interpretation can do in such a situation. We should certainly not attempt to understand the story where the narrator fails, ascribing to it some unrelated meaning, no matter how believable. This would miss the very point that makes this text so special and which we should consider first: the speaker claims to understand nothing of what he says. His nonunderstanding is what must be understood. The narrated story should not be examined for this or that meaning, but we must ask how this incomprehensibility for the speaker might actually be its meaning. We are not so much interested in the content of the story of the chimera carriers but rather in the special way that Baudelaire's text speaks about the narration of the story. If the narrator of the story cannot find meaning in his tale, then it is not altogether clear why he chooses to tell it. In questioning the meaning not only of the story but also of its telling, the rejection of understanding can be seen as the distinguishing characteristic of this text.

CHACUN SA CHIMÈRE

Sous un grand ciel gris, dans une grande plaine poudreuse, sans chemins, sans gazon, sans un chardon, sans une ortie, je rencontrai plusieurs hommes qui marchaient courbés.

Chacun d'eux portait sur son dos une énorme Chimère, aussi

lourde qu'un sac de farine ou de charbon, ou le fourniment d'un fantassin romain.

Mais la monstrueuse bête n'était pas un poids inerte; au contraire, elle enveloppait et opprimait l'homme de ses muscles élastiques et puissants; elle s'agrafait avec ses deux vastes griffes à la poitrine de sa monture; et sa tête fabuleuse surmontait le front de l'homme, comme un de ces casques horribles par lesquels les anciens guerriers espéraient ajouter à la terreur de l'ennemi.

Je questionnai l'un de ces hommes, et je lui demandai où ils allaient ainsi. Il me répondit qu'il n'en savait rien, ni lui, ni les autres; mais qu'évidemment ils allaient quelque part, puisqu'ils étaient poussés par un invincible besoin de marcher.

Chose curieuse à noter: aucun de ces voyageurs n'avait l'air irrité contre la bête féroce suspendue à son cou et collée à son dos; on eût dit qu'il la considérait comme faisant partie de lui-même. Tous ces visages fatigués et sérieux ne témoignaient d'aucun désespoir; sous la coupole spleenétique du ciel, les pieds plongés dans la poussière d'un sol aussi désolé que ce ciel, ils cheminaient avec la physionomie résignée de ceux qui sont condamnés à espérer toujours.

Et le cortège passa à côté de moi et s'enfonça dans l'atmosphère de l'horizon, à l'endroit où la surface arrondie de la planète se dérobe à la curiosité du regard humain.

Et pendant quelques instants je m'obstinai à vouloir comprendre ce mystère; mais bientôt l'irrésistible Indifférence s'abattit sur moi, et j'en fus plus lourdement accablé qu'ils ne l'étaient eux-mêmes par leurs écrasantes Chimères. (I, 282f.)

TO EVERY MAN HIS CHIMERA

Under a vast gray sky, on a vast and dusty plain without paths, without grass, without a nettle or a thistle, I came upon several men bent double as they walked.

Each one carried on his back an enormous Chimera as heavy as a sack of flour, as a sack of coal, as the accoutrement of a Roman foot soldier.

But the monstrous beast was no inanimate weight; on the contrary, it hugged and bore down heavily on the man with its elastic and powerful muscles; it clutched at the breast of its mount with enormous claws; and its fabulous head overhung the man's forehead like those terrible helmets with which ancient warriors tried to strike terror into their enemies.

I questioned one of these men and asked him where they were going like that. He replied that he did not know and that none of them knew; but that obviously they must be going somewhere since they were impelled by an irresistible urge to go on.

A curious thing to note: not one of these travelers seemed to resent the furious beast hanging around his neck and glued to his back; apparently they considered it a part of themselves. All those worn and serious faces showed not the least sign of despair; under the depressing dome of the sky, with their feet deep in the dust of the earth as desolate as the sky, they went along with the resigned look of men who are condemned to hope forever.

And the procession passed by me and disappeared in the haze of the horizon just where the rounded surface of the planet prevents man's gaze from following.

And for a few moments I persisted in trying to understand this mystery; but soon irresistible Indifference descended upon me, and I was more cruelly oppressed by its weight than those men had been by their crushing Chimeras.

HOPE

The chimera, according to French usage, is not only an ancient mythological animal but also represents illusion, the unfounded vision. The men who carry chimeras across the desert are bent over with the weight of illusion. If we ask ourselves what this consists of, then it seems only natural to look for a connection with the journey which the men have undertaken. Asked where they are going, one of them answers that he doesn't know. They are apparently going somewhere, however, since they are driven by an irrepressible force to go on. This line of reasoning is based on an understanding of the journey wherein movement is motivated by the wish to arrive at another place. Movement is seen as directional, that is, towards a goal which gives it meaning. This understanding of movement is maintained in the above argument even though the relationship between movement and goal is notably different from normal, because the goal is unknown. Those who know their goal travel to arrive there. This is impossible for those who don't know where they are going. It is not the intended goal that motivates travel. Travel first postulates a goal. Since I'm traveling, there must be a goal towards which I am heading. If the meaning of movement is seen in the goal, then aimless movement would have no meaning. But since a goal is at least postulated, meaning is only deferred. I may not know where I'm going, but when I arrive, the journey will prove to have been worthwhile. Meaning is given retrospectively to the future arrival. This explains what keeps the chimera carriers going. Their travel to reach a destination from their currently meaningless journey will be given meaning. The meaning of their movement is not present but hoped for. They are driven by the hope for meaning, that is, by the hope for a place that legitimizes the journey which leads to it. The justification for this hope is not doubted by the man who tells about his travels: "but that *obviously* they must be going somewhere since they were impelled by an irresistible urge to go on." This is why they carry with them the hope for meaning, their chimera. They are traveling under an illusion, not because their hope is futile, but because they don't seem to notice its uncertain prospects.

This simple interpretation of hope and chimera does not withstand the sentence that renders the final and complex character of this strange procession: "they walked with the resigned look of men who are condemned to hope forever." The connection that is made between the two contradictory concepts of hope and resignation is difficult. Whoever hopes is not resigned, and whoever is resigned to a given condition does not hope to change it. Baudelaire's chimera carriers hope and are at the same time resigned. The unification of the seemingly disparate is achieved in that hope is the condition to which these men are resigned. The men are content to be condemned to hope. This resignation presumes, however, some distance from their own hope. Those simply hoping would never be able to simultaneously possess the knowledge that hope is a destiny that can never be fulfilled. This is what being condemned to hope means. Hope is instigated by the unsatisfactory conditions in which one finds oneself. Hope is the reference to the future of the unsatisfied. The region through which the hopeful travel is a desert that can only be described by listing what is absent ("without paths, without grass, without a nettle or a thistle"). Those condemned to hope are subjected to eternal desire. Hope is constant, because no satisfaction can quench it. This would be the commutation of the sentence. The chimera carriers are conscious of the unremitting dissatisfaction of the present and their resignation is grounded in this realization. They are content to constantly hope, because there is no point along their path in which need turns into plenty. Their hope is a resigned hope. It is without any positive expectations. The chimera carriers are not traveling towards a definite goal but to somewhere (*quelque part*), to an arbitrary place of which they have no concept except that it is somewhere else. We should therefore not try to understand this hope from the viewpoint of a specific wish. It is not based on future fulfillment but on present need. It is not a hope for what has not yet come to pass but a hope that what is will not always be. It is less a hope for something than away from something. The chimera carriers are not traveling to arrive but to get away. The carrier of their hope is not the to where but the from where. Their world is like the hospital in Baudelaire's *Any Where Out of the World*, where all patients are obsessed with the desire for another bed. "It seems to me that I would always be fine where I am not" (I, 356). Baudelaire's patients and travelers could find a traveling companion in the protagonist of Kafka's story "Der Aufbruch" (The departure), who, asked by his servant about the goal of his imminent journey, answered: "Away from here—that is my goal."

This examination of resigned hope leads to an interpretation of the journey of the chimera carriers that is somewhat contradictory to the previously attempted interpretation. Whereas the movement was at first focused on the goal, it now seems necessary to see it from the perspective of the starting point. The two are complementary, as are hope and resignation. This hope is the hope of getting away; this resignation is the resignation of not arriving. The hope of getting away is necessarily connected with the belief in the possibility of reaching a place that is different from the present one. This rather ill-defined expectation of change is the hope for some future justification of one's own journey. The resignation, on the other hand, depends on this moment's never arriving. Everything always stays the same, and one place is the same as any other. But what else can the motivation of this movement be? We can certainly understand the decision to leave based on the intolerability of the given. We go away because we can't stand it anymore. But somehow the idea is present in our departure that we can stand it somewhere else better. The chimera carriers, who "go on their way with the resigned expression of someone who is condemned to hope eternally," content themselves in the fact that this hope can never be crushed, even though there is absolutely nothing to support it. This unsupported hope for change is the chimera, which drives the travelers on as the unquenchable desire to travel. What is impossible to understand is that, even when we have contented ourselves with the fact that what is hoped for will never be fulfilled, we continue to hope and go our way.

INDIFFERENCE

The procession of travelers is the observer's vision. The observer does not take part in the movement but stands apart and looks on. His distance to what he sees is so great that the earth appears curved. "And the procession passed by me and disappeared in the haze of the horizon just where the rounded surface of the planet prevents man's gaze from following." This could at first be interpreted as the unknown that lies beyond the horizon. We do not know where the chimera carriers' journey will take them. If this were the view of the observer, he would have to hope along with the others, and he would have to go with them to get out of the desert of need. But the picture of the curved earth leads us to another interpretation. The spherical shape of the planet shows the travelers' path to be circular, eventually leading them back to where they started. There is, on the other side of the horizon, nothing new, just the same desert. The perspective encompassing the entire globe is a disillusioned perspective without hope, not full of curiosity. It does not assume that one will forget that one travels in a circle. We come across it again in *Le goût du néant* (The longing for nothingness; I, 76):

> Je contemple d'en haut le globe en sa rondeur
> Et je n'y cherche plus l'abri d'une cahute.

> I contemplate from above the globe in its roundness
> And I no longer seek the shelter of a hut.

In the same poem, the rider Hope and the horse Spirit find each other, and their travels come to an end:

> Morne esprit, autrefois amoureux de la lutte,
> L'Espoir, dont l'éperon attisait ton ardeur,
> Ne veut plus t'enfourcher!

> Gloomy spirit, once in love with battle,
> Hope, whose spur pricked your ardor,
> No longer wants to mount you!

Hope is the force behind movement. The observer stands motionless, because he is without hope.

This hope is a hope for change. Whoever does not have it no longer believes that it is better somewhere else. It makes no difference if he is here or there. The observer in *Chacun sa chimère* is indifferent. Indifference is the absence of difference. Where there is no difference, there is no movement, because in the lack of difference in all things, the difference between here and not here becomes meaningless. The observer stands still. There is no path away from here, because here is the same as there. There are other places, but they are the same as this one. The one for whom here and there are the same is indifferent. Yet this still does not adequately describe indifference. The difficulty of Baudelaire's text lies in the fact that indifference is not just the absence of difference, but that in a certain sense it creates difference. Indifference itself is what distinguishes. The observer is different from the others in that he is indifferent. Indifference is what distinguishes him and makes him different from the chimera carriers. The observer has, in place of the chimera, indifference. In that everything is the same to him, he becomes different. His indifference situates him. This shows that indifference is not all encompassing, because it is itself different from others. Total indifference would be given if the difference between the hopeful and the apathetic did not exist. This would then mean: it makes no difference if I go or stay, if I am condemned to hope or to indifference. The unconquerable drive to go ("l'invincible besoin de marcher") and irresistible indifference ("l'irrésistible Indifférence") would be the same. But this is not at all the case. The distinction between indifference and the chimera remains. In the last sentence, the two are compared but not equated: "I was more cruelly oppressed by its weight than those men had been by their crushing Chimeras." The comparison confirms the difference. Indifference is weightier than the chimera. This means that the observer has not reached a state of complete indifference, but still sees himself in his own indifference as different from the chimera carriers. Recognizing this difference is questioning apathy. Wherever apathy is questioned, however, there exists some interest. The difference between the observer and the chimera carriers is the surviving interest of the apathetic. It appears as a desire to understand that is quickly overcome by apathy. Insofar as the observer is indifferent, he renounces understanding; insofar as indifference makes him different, however, he wants to understand. What he would like to understand is the difference between him and the chimera carriers, who are in the same desert and are driven by an unfounded hope he seems to lack.

At the end, the story and the apathy of the observer become one, but to the extent that the apathy is compared with something else, it recognizes another and is therefore incomplete. It is said of apathy that it is a burden heavier than the chimera. Its greater weight is the difference of apathy towards others. The observer does not succumb to his burden, but he nevertheless sees it as a burden in comparison to other burdens. The heavier something is, the more difficult it is to carry. To the extent that the burden increases, it becomes more unbearable. The observer, who measures the weight of his apathy, does not completely succumb to this weight but experiences in it the unbearable. There is something active in apathy that undermines it. It is accompanied by the sense of not being acceptable and is experienced as a feeling that must be overcome. Those who experience apathy as a burden are already entering into a relationship with it and are therefore already outside it. No matter how apathetic he may be, he is not apathetic towards his apathy. The desire for difference is given to indifference as a heavy burden.

Whoever is no longer apathetic is someone who is interested. Interest highlights certain things and thereby makes them different. The apathetic, however, is incapable of this kind of preference of one thing over another. His lack of interest prevents him from aiming for a certain goal. The desire within his apathy to overcome his apathy has nothing to counter it but is only intent on getting out. Getting away from apathy is instinctual. Each distinct interest is disqualified from apathy. But the fact that apathy can have no interest stirs its interest. Its interest is therefore not directed at this or that but rather at interest itself and the difficulty of having it. Interest is being in the middle. The interested person is caught between where he is and where he is not. His interest lies in establishing the difference between here and there, linked with the desire to get to where this object of interest is. The interest of an apathetic person, on the other hand, is not directed at a thing but at the interest in this thing. Interest as an in-between is the difference of a something and therefore of what separates it. This separation lasts as long as the interest. This is why the person interested in interest as difference never gets anywhere. His interest is endless because it maintains itself as something interested in itself. Those interested in interest are always in between, neither here nor there but on the go. Baudelaire, in his prose poem *Les vocations* (Vocations), uncovered the difference between an interest in something and an interest in interest. The three children, who become what they believe they are supposed to become, are contrasted with a fourth child, who is unable to choose a goal. He would like to travel with the gypsies, who also have no goal. His starting point is *ennui,* which for Baudelaire is the same as apathy, and the purpose of his interest is the interest that keeps him going: "Il m'a souvent semblé que mon plaisir serait d'aller toujours droit devant moi, sans savoir où, sans que personne s'en inquiète, et de voir toujours des pays nouveaux. Je ne suis jamais bien nulle part, et je crois toujours que je serais mieux ailleurs que là où je suis" (It often seemed to me that my pleasure would be always to go straight ahead, without knowing where, without worrying anyone, and always seeing new countries. I am happy nowhere, and I think I will always be happy elsewhere than where I am [I, 334]).

The observer in *Chacun sa chimère* would have to be going somewhere if the interest in interest were a secret force pulling him away from apathy. He would have in himself this incomprehensible, groundless hope that gets the chimera carriers moving, and, contrary to our initial impression, would be one of them. This seems to be contradicted in that the story ends in a disinclination to understand, that is, in indifference.

DISCOURSE

Nothing in the text points to overcoming this indifference, the terminus towards which it flows. But the story does not end there. The text includes not only the story but also its being told. We know of the observer not only what is said about him but also that he is saying it. It is the distinguishing characteristic of first-person narration that the narrator is always a character in his own narration. If the story is told in the past tense, as is the case here, then the narration is subsequent to the narrator. It begins after the story and is its continuation beyond the story's end. The last thing we know about the narrator of *Chacun sa chimère* is not that he succumbs to indifference, but that he becomes a narrator. This leads to the question of how this transition takes place. What makes him talk? One likely incitement to narration might be the need to understand what has happened. The desire retrospectively to provide the past with cohesion and meaning is one credible motivation for such an autobiographical undertaking. But as the narrator begins to tell his story, this motivation becomes obsolete, the attempts at understanding having already been exhausted. The renunciation of understanding may be a part of the story, but nothing supports the assumption that anything has changed in this regard for the narrator. The narration is expressly presented as something not understood. The only thing left is to assume the narration to be a discourse born of indifference. The discourse of the indifferent, unlike the discourse of the interested, serves no purpose. It is not meant to achieve anything beyond itself. Discourse out of indifference is nothing more than discourse away from indifference. As a movement away from . . . , it has no other purpose than to create its own opportunity. The driving force is the interest in the movement itself, that is, the interest in interest, effective in indifference as the sense of its own intolerability.

This detour has not yet made the narrated discourse of *Chacun sa chimère* comprehensible as a discourse born of indifference. It is difficult to understand, based on the manner of discourse, that the story does not gravitate towards a particular purpose, since it is concerned with the transmission of a specific content. What is uncommon about this narration's story is that it is said to be incomprehensible, and the story expressly refuses to understand what it tells. If we want to better understand the uniqueness of this narration born of indifference, then we must ask ourselves what purpose is served by the communication of the incomprehensible. It is difficult to accept that nothing more is to be gained from the text than the incomprehensibility of what is said. We can pose the question from the perspective of what is communicated, that is, from the standpoint of the chimera carriers, the story's main subject.

The reader's first and most urgent question of *Chacun sa chimère* concerns the meaning of the chimera carriers. It is also the narrator's question, a question he cannot answer and finally refuses to try. This not only does not answer the question, but makes it even more troubling. Considering the text's refusal to answer, the question becomes to what extent the meaning of the chimera carriers can be understood. The comments already made on this subject have shown the internal contradictions of the chimera carriers, whose attitude bespeaks both hope and resignation and who, in the end, remain an enigma in the simultaneity of the irreconcilable. Regarding the meaning of a story whose content is incomprehensible, we must first question the meaning of the failure to understand the meaning of the chimera carriers. The chimera carriers lose none of their effectiveness through the obscurity of their meaning. The reader's sense of the chimera carriers is obviously based on something other than a definite meaning. This other can be better viewed from the perspective of contradiction, given considerable weight in the text. This contradiction is not only expressed in the opposition of hope and resignation but also in the contrast between the appearance of the chimeras and the facial expressions of the men who carry them. The head of the chimera, as it appears over each man's head, is described in terms of the intimidating headgear of ancient warriors: "its fabulous head overhung the man's forehead like those horrible helmets with which ancient warriors tried to strike terror into their enemies." Baudelaire's interest in helmets is based not only on Manet's sketch, in which the poet is barely recognizable under a huge top hat, but also on his plan for an "elègie des chapeaux," which appears as one of his unrealized projects for prose poems. A draft version speaks of the relationship between hats and heads: "The hats remind one of heads and seem like a gallery of heads. For each hat, by its character, calls for a head and reveals spirit to the eyes" (I, 373). The hat points to the face that best suits it, just as each face demands a suitable hat. In *Chacun sa chimère*, the face under the frightening chimera helmet is characterized by fatigue and resignation. Hat and face act as hope and resignation, visible in the dichotomous appearance of the chimera carriers. But hope is the absence of resignation and vice versa, so that hope and resignation both point to their own absence, even though both are still present. This internal contradiction of the chimera carriers is their incomprehensibility. It is impossible to separate the chimera and the men as contradictions. Both must expressly be seen as a whole ("they considered it a part of themselves"). The question of the meaning of the chimera carriers is the question of the meaning of this whole. The whole is a reference, but since it is itself made up of a contradictory referential structure, the reference can never achieve its purpose but remains suspended in the openness of contradiction. The reference cannot be a reference to . . . but must be understood as a reference from. . . . The chimera carriers have meaning in that they point away from themselves, that is, they never achieve meaning in the sense of something signified. Their meaning is their signification.

The story tells about chimera carriers. The narration is a discourse of indifference. Its relationship with what it expresses is now apparent; it is not a discourse that wants to understand. Its purpose is therefore not the discovery of meaning. If what is said were to be given this or that meaning, then the discourse would be one that understands. Here it is born of indifference as the renunciation of wanting to understand. This discourse does not speak the meaning of the chimera carriers themselves but the chimera carriers as carriers of meaning. Something is said that has meaning, but the meaning remains hidden. What is spoken in the discourse thereby becomes a metaphor for its expression. The expression of the poem is like the chimera carriers as something said, a signification not given by the meaning. Its meaning is not what it means but the distance from . . . , its meaning. Giving meaning as the meaning of the expression can only be expressed so that the expressed in turn becomes a signifier without arriving at a meaning. The chimera carriers are this expressed signifier, which can be considered as the self-representation of the indifferent narrative discourse. That the chimera carriers move at all is as incomprehensible as the narrator's discourse. Both are attributable in the end to the compelling grip of the chimeralike, from which no manner of lucidity can protect us. The highest lucidity is not what claims to eliminate the chimeralike but rather what recognizes it. This is the lucidity of those resigned in hope and speaking in indifference.

UNDERSTANDING

If this has brought us a certain understanding of Baudelaire's text, this understanding itself is the least understood because in the poem itself, understanding is not reached. It is most disconcerting, especially in the reading of this prose poem, that all attempts at understanding prove fruitless. Before we ask about ways to understand the text, we must question the understanding that confronts us in the text. The narrator, concerned at first with understanding, sinks into apathy. Understanding would have consisted of discovering the meaning of the chimera carriers. The indifference in which the will to understand is extinguished is the indifference to the meaning of the meaningful. A reduction of what gives meaning to something meant through it is avoided. It is, however, not altogether certain that all understanding is thereby denied. If it is true that the chimera carriers do not mean this or that but are signification itself, then we might come closest if we reject any determination of their meaning. This approach can also be seen as a form of understanding. The text provides answers as to how this understanding comes about. The desire to understand is replaced with narration. In realizing the impossibility of communicating the meaning of the chimera carriers, the narration becomes an understanding of them as signifiers. This understanding is not, however, an expression of some thing. The meaningful, whose meaning remains inaccessible, is understood in the conversion to the act of narration, whose signification remains as unreducible as that of the narrative. Signification, as the chimera carriers are to be understood, occurs in narration. The interpretation and expression of the meaning of what we encounter as meaningful is rejected. The narration, whose signification remains as irreducible as that of the discourse in the sense that within it occurs the act of signification, that is, what is to be understood. Narration out of indifference to the signified, as occurring signification, is as close as we can get to the elusive signification it narrates. The understanding of signification occurs as the signification of narration.

This understanding, as it occurs in the text, can be better defined if it is related to our present attempt to understand the text. This attempt has up to now concentrated on the determination of meaning. From this we have seen that what the text communicates cannot be defined as a determinable meaning but is to be seen as something meaningful. This interpretation defines signification as the meaning of what is communicated. This is the common understanding that is denied us by the text, because it cannot succeed. What we found as the meaning of the communicated is nevertheless noteworthy. The special thing about this meaning is that it is signification. The text thereby shows itself to be a special kind of discourse. What it expresses does not refer beyond itself but back to itself. It is self-referential discourse. This reference is not accomplished in that the discourse expresses itself. Instead, the discourse expresses something that refers back to itself. The story of the chimera carriers is told. They are, as what is expressed in the discourse, a figure for their own expression. But why such a roundabout way via figurative speech? The discourse can only express itself as something expressing by turning itself into its own expression. In that it becomes its own expression, it slips away from itself as something expressing. It loses itself in the expression it becomes. It can regain itself if it expresses something that simultaneously refers away from itself, without having the reference resolved in a particular. The reference that is unresolved in its own reference refers back to the discourse of which it is the expression. Self-reference is therefore necessarily figurative, because only a figure allows the relationship between expressing and expression to be expressed as a whole, without having the expressing slip away completely in what has been expressed. The text accomplishes the reference to itself as expressing something about a common communication. What is thereby communicated prevents, through the suspension of its own meaning, the act of signification and expressing from being forgotten. In that what has been expressed in the discourse refers back to itself, it avoids the danger of losing itself in what it expresses.

Given this kind of textual understanding, we must ask ourselves at this juncture if there is still room for the interpretation that has led us to this understanding. The text seems to create its own understanding as discourse in self-reference, requiring no further interpretation. Nevertheless, the self-understanding of the text is made possible through interpretation. The function of interpretation might be seen in the necessarily figurative character of self-referential discourse not being recognized as such. Nothing in the text protects it from a reading that is hungry for meaning and fixes a discourse's expression and signifying. The proposed interpretation would like to prevent such a misunderstanding by showing expression and signification to be the meaning of the text. It can only do this by reducing the figurativeness of the text and expressing directly what the text expresses indirectly. Interpretive discourse then runs into exactly the same trouble that was avoided by the interpreted text through figurative speech. Interpretation can only speak of discourse and signification to the extent that it objectifies the discourse, losing it and itself in the act. Insofar as interpretation forgets its own active character, it becomes inadequate for the text at hand, itself concerned with avoiding this falling into the expressed. To be adequate, interpretive discourse would have to speak figuratively, in which case it would be prone to the same misunderstandings that it sets out to clear up.

If literary discourse can be considered as a discourse concerned with itself, then the conflict that raises its head becomes valid for all discourse on literature. This discourse can itself be literature. It then understands the discourse to which it refers in that it realizes the discourse in the very same act. This is the understanding realized in *Chacun sa chimère*: the transformation of the signification of the chimera carriers in the act of narration. The narrative act, which represents itself in the narration, understands in that it is what it narrates: narrative and its narration in one. But this understanding cannot, although it takes place through some communication, end in the communication of what is understood, because the discursive act is never available, only realizable. This would mean that literature is only comprehensible in that we create it. We can understand it to the extent that we avoid saying what it is. An understanding of literature can only exist *within* literature. This is opposed by the other kind of understanding that is always forced to some degree into objectifying literature. It is the kind of understanding that the narrator of *Chacun sa chimère* rejects but that the

interpretation uses to be able to express signification as the meaning of what has been expressed. Interpretive discourse thereby
distances itself from the text and contradicts itself. It is bound to
express what the text in question is prevented from expressing. Its
legitimacy may lie in the fact that it succeeds. But it succeeds at the
cost of its own self-understanding, something the literary text
already has. Interpretive discourse does exactly what it attempts to
prevent. It wants to save the text from being fixed to a specific
meaning and preserve in the text the productivity of continuous
meaning. But to express what the text does, it must do precisely
what the text avoids doing to do what it cannot express. Signification was understood in that it hardened into meaning, because it
had to be expressed and made accessible to the kind of understanding that the text avoids, allowing the act of signification and
expression to take place. Conversely, interpretive discourse, in that
it illuminated the discursive act in contrast with what has been
expressed, was also the negation of its own insufficiency. The
emphasis of the discursive act on the level of what has been
expressed is contrary to the discursive style of communication,
where the expression disappears in what has been expressed. The
content of what is communicated was the questioning of communicative discourse. Here we seem to see glimpses of a relationship
between Baudelaire's text and interpretive discourse. In both, what
has been expressed refers to the act of its being expressed. In
Chacun sa chimère, this self-reference results from the incomprehensibility of what is communicated. In interpretive discourse, this
results from the contradiction between what is communicated and
the communication. But this similarity remains illusory. In *Chacun
sa chimère*, the renunciation of understanding, as the indication of
the impossibility of ever reducing the meaningful to a specific
meaning, is built into the text. The contradiction in interpretive
discourse between communicating and what is communicated is
not reflected in such a discourse unless it were to step outside itself,
as it has in this case. Interpretive discourse is prevented from
continuously being concerned with itself by its fundamental focus
on the object. If it were able to show more concern for itself, it

could more closely approach its object—the text as the relationship between discursive act and content—but at the cost of being able to make any assertions concerning the text. It would then no longer be interpretation but literature. That it might be able to unify the two: that is, each beyond itself and away from itself—but to where?—is the chimeralike hope it carries.

Rimbaud

"JE EST UN AUTRE"

Disputed Aesthetics

The letter containing the phrase "JE est un autre" is polemical, and the phrase is intended to be shocking. The phrase challenges the domination of the subject as the foundation of an aesthetics that celebrates works of art as free products of responsible authorities. "Legally, art can only be defined as a product of freedom, that is, of a choice whose actions are based on reason" (Kant, *Critique of Judgment*, § 43). The I is not a romantic aesthetic, but in a romantic aesthetic the I is itself and in control. Conversely, the subject, aware of its otherness, loses control and remains at best a perceptive observer of events. But the disempowerment of the subject in the phrase "JE est un autre" goes along with its employment in an elevated self-awareness. The idea of the I as a preeminent authority is precisely the illusion that the phrase shows to be untenable. A better insight into the process of poetic discourse cannot be the basis for the same domination it rejects. But it does make it—but what does that mean?—more accessible in its uncontrollability. The poet's self-awareness is the awareness of his own discourse's detachment.

Context

The phrase, in which I is another, stands in contrast like a colored dot on a gray background. It has always been preserved by its readers in isolation. It exudes a power not shared by its surroundings to which we succumb before we understand. This phrase overpowers us, and the experience it reports becomes the experience of the report. We are justified in asking from where this phrase gains such power. It is also justified to ask what kind of understanding this surrender to its fascination allows. Is there any guarantee that this phrase will have this effect, and wouldn't we have to examine this passage in the context of the letter to determine what it says? The need to read in context stems from the question of "how it might be meant." The opinionated authority is a speaker who has access to language and uses it to express his opinion. The question of meaning conflicts with the cited phrase, because it presumes a control of discourse that this phrase destroys. The isolation of the phrase corresponds to its sense and allows it to take effect without questioning what it is *supposed* to say. "JE est un autre" is not meant one way or another but occurs as the transformation of the speaker, whose opinion is lost. Even though the force of the phrase lies in its expression, it is nevertheless a statement whose expression explains the correlation as well as being explained by it.

Change

That I is an other is expressed in a discourse on poetic discourse. Disputed is the primacy of the speaker over what is spoken. When I speak, then it is not I who am speaking. We are concerned here with the discursive authority. This cannot be solved by the replacement of I by an other. If an other were to speak in my place, then it would simply be a different I. We are not questioning this or that person as the discursive authority but rather the subjectivity of discourse in general. Whatever speaks is not a different I but is different with regard to every I. Whenever speech takes place, it speaks not without me, but the I is transformed to the other in speaking. The I is, whenever it speaks, always already the other. I does not precede the discourse; it is within it. There is no decidable I that is present and that begins to speak. In speaking it gives up control and surrenders to language. I transpires as something speaking. As something taking place in discourse, the I would have to be able to gain control over itself in discourse, to understand itself as speaking, and to find itself in speaking. I does not find itself as something that it always was and perhaps didn't know, because it wasn't itself before it began speaking. I only becomes itself in that it transpires in speaking, and it can therefore only find itself as what it has yet to become in speaking. In speaking, the I consigns itself to language as something uncontrollable. It finds itself by leaving itself. It finds itself in change. This is not an arbitrary process, in which I remains the same although it changes itself. The I is the changed, and what effects this change is the other. The one who wants to change himself is not the one who says I am an other but rather the one who experiences himself most strongly as himself when he feels himself slipping into the other. Discourse is the experience of this slipping away. My speaking changes me, because what is supposedly mine is effective as the other, to which I belong, although it is not essentially the I in which I must lose myself to become myself.

Uncontrollability

The phrase "JE est un autre" speaks of the speaker's crumbling domination of his own discourse. The controlled discourse would presume an independent authority from which it could be derived. As something controlled, it would be secondary to whatever is in control. It would be available, would be used, and would therefore always be instrumental. Should there be a noninstrumental concept of language, then we must abandon any authority primary to discourse. Noninstrumental discourse is uncontrolled. Language is not used in it, but the speaker exposes himself to it. The speaker does not know what uncontrolled discourse expresses, because its expression is neither subordinate to him nor can it be traced back to him. The uncontrollability of what is expressed is not only valid for the speaker but also for the receiver, who, to understand the discourse, must make it his own. In the attempt to do this, he encounters the impossibility of possession. The uncontrollability of what has been said prevents the determination of discourse. Any

determination of discourse to something expressed would make
the expressed impotent. Conversely, the more original expression,
in contrast to all the speaker's attempts at communication, is felt in
the unavailability of what is expressed. Whoever attempts to speak
surrenders to this expression. The need for the controlled statement comes from the fear of surrendering to language. We don't
know where it will lead us, abduct us, or seduce us. The poet is the
one who endures the risk of the unknown by changing himself in
speaking, letting language do the talking. "He reaches the unknown, and when, crazed, he was about to lose the intelligibility of
his visions, he saw them! May he collapse in his boundings from
things unnameable and unheard of" (*Oeuvres complètes*, 271). The
unheard and unnameable is what has always been the lost and
disavowed, although active, expression and is effective in the un-
premeditation in all its discourse.

Expression and Expressed

The phrase "JE est un autre" is an insight into the detachment of
speaking. But isn't detachment, in that it is expressed, controlled
and thereby eliminated? The attempt to express the uncontrollability of discourse aims to control it. It is to be silenced in the
solidification of what is expressed. As something expressed, uncontrollability is brought under control. The phrase "JE est un autre"
contradicts what it expresses, unless it were a discourse that admit-
ted its own uncontrollability. We must ask how this phrase relates
to what it expresses. Does its expression of the speaker's I hold true
for anyone expressing this phrase? Is the subject of the sentence
(JE) also the subject—the discursive authority—of the discourse in
which the phrase occurs? Does the statement "JE est un autre" take
place in the illusion of being controlled, or does it lose itself in the
uncontrollability it expresses? If the phrase does not understand
itself to be a determining statement, then it must unexpress what
has been expressed. This unexpression, as the rejection of control
over discourse, would be the speaker's personal task as the discursive authority. But the discourse is not uncontrolled when the
speaker expressly forgoes controlling it, rather, when it slips away

from him. Rejection is not the speaker's accomplishment but his subjugation by language. This is evidenced as the undecidability of discourse that cannot be fixed in a specific expression. The opinion of the speaker dims in the face of undecidability, and discourse opens itself to the unpremeditated expression that makes it possible in the first place. The phrase "JE est un autre" is not decidable in one important respect. JE is distinguished above all other words through capitalization. What does this emphasize? If I were the speaker, then the phrase would have to be: "je suis un autre." If I were the object of the phrase, then we would expect: "le moi est un autre." Both versions lack the tension of Rimbaud's phrase. I am an other: this is the private determination of the speaker's otherness. Nothing in this manner of speech points to the difficulty of a statement that conflicts with what it says. The person who claims to be someone else does so as someone saying *I*, thereby reversing the claimed change in its pronouncement. Conversely, if an other is meant by "the I," then no one comes forward to be recognized as the speaker. The I in this sentence is the objectified subject that allows itself to be spoken of. The suggestion that everything that is said has to be attributed to a silent *I*, which enables all discourse, cannot be claimed for a discourse that strives to subordinate expression to the expressed. The sentence speaks differently: "JE est un autre." JE is associated in such a way—and this must be emphasized—that it is both the speaker and the object and neither of them. The phrase remains suspended between both versions, defines it one way or another, and thereby deflates it. Someone appears in the phrase as the speaker (JE) but then fails to speak. The first person is combined with the third person in such a way that makes it impossible for us to decide for one or the other. The discourse proceeds in such a way that I, which posits itself and is recognizable as the speaking authority, slips away from itself, errs and changes from "I am" to "I is." It is detached from itself and undermines itself as the speaking authority. This undermining is not the expressed of the phrase. It is what the phrase occurs as. "JE est un autre" is neither my discourse nor discourse about the I but discourse that is realized as the change of JE. The phrase speaks in a way that robs me, who speaks it, of power over it. Its power is based on a privation of power, and what I was falls headlong into it.

Theater

No one speaks. JE is not the speaker, because it is no longer the first person and no longer I. I as the first person of the verb is always doubly determined, on the one hand by what the discourse says about it, on the other hand as the one who says it. I, with whatever verb it may join itself, always means: I say. I am an other includes: I say, that I am. "JE est . . ." is the rejection of "I say." JE is, contrary to its placement before the verb, not the I that says. Here JE is said, without having defined the discursive authority as the discourse's reduction. The renunciation of the speaker is not his negation, something still bound to a viewpoint and forced to reintroduce the negated in the act of negation. JE in "JE est un autre" is not negated but is blurred in the haze of its own ambiguity (I am / the I is). There is no other viewpoint, such as that of the other, to counter that of the "I say." It dissolves midway, there where the speaker languishes, and lets language happen. This letting happen in the middle of viewlessness is the theater in Rimbaud's text. "I attend the hatching of my thought: I look at it, I listen to it: I release my bow: the symphony makes its rustle in the depths or comes from a leap onto the stage" (270). I is not only the audience in this theater ("j'assiste," "je regarde," "j'écoute"), but also the piece that is being played ("l'éclosion de ma pensée") and the stage ("la scène") on which the production takes place. The mind produces the thinking which it then watches and observes. This watching oneself is self-awareness. But according to the theater's explanation of our phrase, I am an other. To be self-aware does not mean that one possesses oneself through consciousness. I myself is not a first and final authority that guarantees consciousness. There is a hole in the seemingly sound system of self-reference through which the un-controllable other streams in and destroys the self-assurance of I. The play that I watch is my thinking, but what appears in my thinking as my thought is not I. I may be my own play, but the one I see as myself is an other. I walk next to myself and encounter

myself as a stranger, whose actions, whether they surprise, enter-
tain, or astonish me, are not subject to my influence. Self-awareness is the observer's awareness of the self, knowing that what he
sees is himself but that it all happens without him. Self-awareness is
the awareness of being an other, of being isolated from oneself; it
is the awareness of the other in me. The other is isolated in
this awareness as something inaccessible. To the extent that with
this self-awareness goes the awareness of what cannot be reached
through awareness, the I cannot be reduced to an awareness. Self-
awareness is not only an awareness of an awareness. It is also the
realization of the I in the impossibility of self-containment within
the framework of this awareness. I can only be itself in that it lets
itself go, opening itself to something more fundamental than the
inclusive awareness of itself. Rimbaud's theater is therefore not a
self-production of something in control of itself but an encounter
of something that changes itself with the other within.

Conversation

Within me is the other, experienced as something withdrawn.
Rimbaud's text speaks of "my thinking," whose unfolding I wit-
ness. It is not clear, however, to what extent my thinking is withdrawn from me. Should we consider here things from the dark that
step into the light as thought? Something thought becomes accessible by being thought. What was previously detached becomes
conscious and accessible as thinking unfolds. The detachment of
what is thought is therefore inconsequential, because it can be
remedied. There is no real control over what is brought into the
light of thinking, but whatever comes into that light is established
in a comforting objectivity. Not the contents of thinking are
withdrawn, but rather the thinking itself. "It's wrong to say: I
think. One should rather say: they think me" (268). The fact that
thinking occurs is what is beyond myself, within me. Rimbaud
believed openness to the impossibility to influence the thought
process to be the poet's distinguishing characteristic. The poet not
only has a sense for the content of thinking and discourse but also
for the incomprehensibility of the origin of thinking and discourse,

isolated from his own grasp. Again and again, thinking and expression are buried under the rubble of what is thought and expressed. Letting it shine through nonetheless is the accomplishment of a discourse that does not fall victim to instrumentality. It remains open to the unvanquished within itself and allows it free rein. The conversation in Rimbaud's poetry is often realized and appropriate to his theater, because in it everything is said with a view to letting the other have its say.

CONVERSATION ABOUT
A CONVERSATION
   (Myself, the Other)

> L'ETERNITÉ
>
> Elle est retrouvée.
> Quoi?—L'Eternité.
> C'est la mer allée
> Avec le soleil.
>
> Ame sentinelle,
> Murmurons l'aveu
> De la nuit si nulle
> Et du jour en feu.
>
> Des humains suffrages,
> Des communs élans
> Là tu te dégages
> Et voles selon.
>
> Puisque de vous seules,
> Braise de satin,
> Le Devoir s'exhale
> Sans qu'on dise: enfin.
>
> Là pas d'espérance,
> Nul orietur.
> Science avec patience,
> Le supplice est sûr.
>
> Elle est retrouvée.
> Quoi?—L'Eternité.

C'est la mer allée
Avec le soleil. (133f.)

She is rediscovered.

What? Eternity.
It's the sea gone down
With the sun.

Sentinel soul,
Let's murmur the wish
Of nothing night
And day on fire.

From human approvals,
From common impulses,
Here you free yourself
And fly in accordance.

Since from you alone,
Embers of satin,
Duty is breathed
With no one saying: at last.

Here no hope,
No *orietur.*
Science with patience,
The torment is sure.

She is rediscovered.
What? Eternity.

It's the sea gone down
With the sun.

MYSELF: She is rediscovered.
THE OTHER: What?
MYSELF: Eternity.
THE OTHER: Why didn't you say so to begin with?
MYSELF: I ask myself why it isn't said right away, I mean, in the poem, where our conversation takes place. In any case, our conversation would never have gotten started if I had said at the beginning what *she* meant. You wouldn't have had to ask. Our conver-

sation would have been superfluous. It would only have been necessary if my account were incomplete. You were obviously angry when you reproached me for not having said everything right away. Your question was meant as a criticism, wasn't it?

THE OTHER: You always seem to be primarily concerned with how something is meant. But I must admit that I don't understand my own question anymore. If your explanation of our conversation is right, then I shouldn't have posed the question. I would like to think that my first question arose out of curiosity: to find out what is rediscovered. But after you informed me on that account, the conversation should really have been over, because then I knew what it was you wanted to say. We had arrived at the same place, just as if you had told me from the beginning that eternity is rediscovered. And yet—this is what concerns *me*—we hadn't both arrived at the same place. The phrase "eternity is rediscovered" could have given me cause to ask you a number of things (which I might still do later). For example, how eternity is lost and how it can be rediscovered. I could never have asked the way I did: why didn't you say so to start with? This question really doesn't belong to our initial conversation anymore but actually starts another one that is connected to the first. We're not talking about eternity anymore and what happens to it—and somehow I'm glad about that—but rather about the conversation we had about it. And that's why, you see, we are not at the same place, as we otherwise would have been. It could have changed with a single bit of information. But because your statement was incomplete and required an exchange of words, we've gotten away from what you thought you were saying and have concentrated on the saying itself. Is that what you wanted?

MYSELF: Now you're asking how it was meant. I don't know. I would like to know how to interpret the dialogue in Rimbaud's poem: "Elle est retrouvée / Quoi?—L'Eternité." We would have to pass your question on to the poem. It would sound something like: why does the first person in the conversation hide what he has found?

THE OTHER: You're making it too easy on yourself. You are this first person, and your question is directed at him.

MYSELF: You're being difficult. I'd rather be alone. Secondary literature would be better served. But since you're here, I'll fill you in on why I hid what I had found: I didn't want to tell you because . . .

THE OTHER: But you did say it.

MYSELF: But only after you had asked me. I have to admit I changed my mind and decided to tell you.

THE OTHER: At least this gives our conversation some purpose. It doesn't happen every day that someone changes his mind. It's even rarer when he admits it, even begrudgingly. But why begrudgingly? Because we are, after all, primarily someone based on our opinions, that is, we are what we appear to be. We don't like to question ourselves. That's why I wonder if you're telling the truth when you claim that you didn't want to disclose what was found. That way, you still have the chance to disclose it if you want to. Since you really did disclose it, you have to admit to having changed your mind, but at least you had an opinion. You seem to think that's better than not having one at all, because there was nothing on which it could be based. Isn't it true that you didn't even know what had been rediscovered?

MYSELF: But I said what it was.

THE OTHER: Only after I asked.

MYSELF: But I couldn't have said "*She* is rediscovered" if I didn't already know that what had been found was feminine.

THE OTHER: Since we're not talking about eternity, we don't need to be concerned with her gender. But wasn't this feminine gender the only thing that was certain from the beginning?

MYSELF: Nothing gets past you, does it?

THE OTHER: It's not hidden at all but clear as day. Just think back to your own words: "She is rediscovered." We only need to stick to what the sentence tells us. It isn't eternity but a feminine pronoun. We don't have anything else at the beginning of the poem. It doesn't start with the name of a thing but rather with a word that stands for the missing thing that isn't discovered until later on in the conversation. Everyone who takes in what Rimbaud wrote and what we have said has to see that what was claimed to be found in the first sentence is in reality what was searched for, and the conversation is its discovery. Only because we're used to accepting pronouns as standing for something else, and we assume that what they stand for is already present, do we then assume that *she* stands for something known. But this isn't getting us anywhere. If the speaker knows what the pronoun stands for, then why doesn't he just say it? It seems to me much more likely that he doesn't know what he's talking about.

MYSELF: Then I have to ask myself why you asked me something that you assumed I didn't know.

THE OTHER: To let you find it. The question was unavoidable. It didn't just arbitrarily follow your sentence. If I hear that *she* is rediscovered, then I have to ask what it is that is found. *She* is rediscovered: this provokes a question, it is said with the question in mind. To such an extent that the question is more yours than mine. The necessity that lies in the pronoun *she* is expressed. This pronoun is not something after the fact, but something that looks ahead. It is an agenda that must be satisfied without already knowing how. It questions what it stands for. This question is the driving force behind the incomplete statement and is what started our conversation. By asking the question that was inherent in your sentence, I gave you the chance to disclose what the pronoun referred to.

MYSELF: It isn't easy to follow your train of thought, and I have to abandon notions I would like to have of myself. I would always have liked to have been known as someone who only speaks when he has something to say. You are implying that I speak not because but rather in order to have something to say. Only by speaking do I become someone who might in retrospect be able to say about himself that he had something to say. But even if I content myself with that, plenty of problems remain. You define our conversation as a search for what is found. If, however, we proceed from my first, albeit incomplete, sentence, "She is rediscovered," and see in it the question you consequently asked, then the answer to this question is given and limited only to a very broad framework. What is found could be my watch or my girlfriend. Any feminine noun would do. Why does it have to be eternity? We can't get that from the flow of the conversation.

THE OTHER: It seems that we do finally have to talk about eternity. I was always a little afraid that it would come to this. It's true that I can't explain eternity.

MYSELF: How would it be if we assumed that I knew from the very beginning what I was talking about?

THE OTHER: That's fine with me.

MYSELF: You're going to give up your position that easily?

THE OTHER: That's why we're here. Have you considered why the one who lets us speak is writing a dialogue instead of an essay? I think he needs us to help him get by without a viewpoint. He realized that there is always speaking before anything is spoken and that one can't approach a discourse that does more than just make statements with more statements. This is only possible in giving up the position from which statements are made. In a dialogue there are at least two viewpoints that question one another, and it's difficult to attribute a dialogue like ours or the one in Rimbaud's poem to an author, because we never really know where he stands. If, however, we are thought of as viewpoints that undermine the other, then nothing prevents us from doing away with a determination and questioning our own positions. That's why I don't mind at all suddenly admitting that you always knew what the pronoun in the first sentence stood for. But you have to explain to me why you kept it a secret.

MYSELF: The last time I tried, you interrupted me. But I'll be happy to try again. I said that I didn't name what was found, because I didn't want to. I didn't want to give it a name because it seemed to me that by doing so I would lose it. Since I've long since lost eternity again, I don't have to be afraid of finally talking about it. Eternity is not something you have, but something you are in. Finding is becoming. This is why, in a text I would gladly explain to you, Rimbaud talked about his "eternal life." "A cette [période, c'était] c'était ma vie éternelle, non écrite, non chantée, —quelque chose comme la Providence [les lois du monde un] à laquelle on croit et qui ne chante pas" (At this [time, it was] it was my eternal life, unwritten, unsung, —something like Providence [laws of the world one] in which one believes and which does not sing [249]).

THE OTHER: That's a draft of *Une saison en enfer* (A season in hell). Ignoring the fact that it's a discarded draft, it seems to me to be one of those texts that everyone does with what they want, because they speak so undecidably that a lot can be read into them, and very little can be refuted.

MYSELF: Is that so bad? The fact that we're talking about a draft doesn't prevent us from taking it seriously. It doesn't undo the fact that something was spoken, but it does give what is said a preliminary nature that can never be recalled and that protects it from solidifying. You really ought to have some sense for this, since you wanted to read the sentence "She is rediscovered" as a draft.

THE OTHER: I'd like to come back to that later. Right now, let's stick with eternity.

MYSELF: Gladly. I believe that, in the text I read, Rimbaud tries to describe or circumscribe what he calls his eternal life. But it is this writing that contradicts an eternity that is unwritten and unsung. Whoever speaks of eternity has already lost it, is no longer in it, but rather at a distance that allows him to talk about it. Any amount of speaking is too much here. When I said "It is rediscovered," I not only said too little, as you thought, but too much, because whoever claims to have found eternity loses it by saying so. I was cautious because I sensed this. I didn't want to identify eternity, so I could preserve it.

THE OTHER: Then I guess I shouldn't have asked . . .

MYSELF: On the contrary. I needed your question. Only I took it differently from what you apparently intended. I don't know that I said too little, but I think I said too much. That's why I don't take the question as a desire for additional information but as questioning the statement I made in spite of everything. The question raises doubts about the assertion. It reestablishes the openness that the assertion closed off. In that your question eliminated the excessive-ness of my discourse, it allowed me to rediscover what might have been lost, what I said I had rediscovered: eternity. "L'Eternité": this was not simply an answer to a question; it was the scream I let out as I ran through the hole you made in the linguistic concrete. I discovered eternity in the dissolution of the sentence, in the blurring of boundaries, and in the disappearance of appearance: "C'est la mer allée / Avec le soleil."

THE OTHER: I didn't think you had that kind of rhetoric in you. May I nevertheless ask the sobering question whether you now think my interpretation of our conversation is refuted?

MYSELF: I don't want to make it that easy. I just found out from you that it doesn't do much good to insist on viewpoints and opinions. Each of us has explained our dialogue in his own way. Our opinions confront each other, and now they question themselves. We can't go back past the stage we have reached. We shouldn't argue over who's right. Since both explanations are possible, we're both right. The amazing thing is not that we disagree, but that our conversation—or, if you prefer, Rimbaud's poem—which we would like to understand, allows for our disagreement. It is, so to speak, the higher unification of disunity, since it is, in the end, a single word that is the cause of our disagreement. It seems to me that we should try to see our differing interpretations in light of the unity of the interpreted conversation, instead of talking ourselves apart again.

THE OTHER: I hope that doesn't lead to our convergence. It would be unfortunate if our conversation were to end so suddenly. But since the text in which we are supposed to converge is still the conversation from which we were created, we might be granted some additional time. Be that as it may, our explanations of the dialogue undeniably have something in common. The conversation is a discovery for both of us. What else could a conversation be? The fact that it takes place only makes sense if it cannot be replaced by a simple statement, such as: eternity is rediscovered. The conversation is the discovery that might later result in a statement but that cannot be replaced in the actuality of its transpiration. Maybe this will bring us back to the draft.

MYSELF: We seem to be constantly changing roles. We should probably be content with the fact that we belong together. But you wanted to say something about the draft.

THE OTHER: Right. It occurred to me that foresight comes into play. You didn't say anything about it, but foresight is employed in, even equated with, "eternal life." But isn't foresight primarily a draft? We tend to think of it as premonition, which we, since we don't have it ourselves, tend to ascribe to some divinity. Our human foresight is no less foresight just because it isn't divine omniscience. It is not the knowing foresight of the draft. This is the distinguishing characteristic of the draft: we don't know how it will turn out, but still we work to realize it, because somehow we foresee it. Without this foresight, nothing would ever be drafted; and no draft would take the risk that a real draft does if foresight were certain. If we knew from the beginning how what has yet to be created would finally turn out, we wouldn't have to create it. And so I take our conversation to be a draft. It is not the refashioning of some statement into dialogue form. It takes the risk of a not-knowing, searching foresight. Only because the conversation searches can we understand it as discovery.

MYSELF: Maybe now we understand the foresight in the draft better, which incited you to yours. Rimbaud says that his "eternal life" is "something like Providence in which one believes and which does not sing." This means that eternity is discovered by whomever believes in this nonsinging foresight. Foresight doesn't sing because it is the foresight of song. Song is the draft made possible by foresight. Rimbaud's eternal life is the belief in the unlimited ability to draft, the carefree openness to the unforeseen in one's own foresight. "De joie, je devins un opéra fabuleux" (What joy! I myself became a fabulous work [249]). In this way, whoever lets himself speak presents himself as himself—as the other.

THE OTHER: That must be me. In me you go beyond yourself. Eternal is the life that is, in the foresight of itself, no longer itself, but the potential and the draft of the other's song, which it is not.

MYSELF: You were right in not wanting to talk about eternity. But let's think about the draft again. If it is what you say it is—and I must admit, I can't imagine it as anything else—then what is created if we complete our drafts is never quite what we wanted, unless it was from the start not quite subject to our will. The unforeseen always lurks in the draft and participates in the creation of the nascent. But then none of our work is really quite our own. Since our foresight is not knowing, we are not authors. "JE est un autre."

THE OTHER: That's me again, if I may say so myself. The fact that you open yourself up to me and I to you makes our conversation a draft. Each one of us is the inestimable in the foresight of the other. It is rediscovered. What is? Eternity. Each of us understands it differently. *You* believe to possess something that you lose in speaking and regain in the dissolution of discourse. *I* believe that nothing is already present and that discourse brings out what it offers. Holding a conversation both ways shows that neither of us is master of a conversation in which the other is unforeseeably active. You discover what you say in speaking, and you lose it by saying it. Then you're forced to dissolve the present discourse. Our conversation has taught us that much. It doesn't matter so much that we interpret the dialogue differently, but rather that each one discovers the other's interpretation by doing so. Each of us is the risk in the other's draft. That he takes the risk and puts it into words allows him to discover in his discourse what he didn't want to say but is still said as the contribution of the other. We are always together as draftsmen.

Hölderlin

Hölderlin and Rousseau

Pausanias: O Sohn des Himmels!
Empedokles: Ich war es! ja! und möcht es nun erzählen.
          — Hölderlin, *Sämtliche Werke* (4, 106f.)

Pausanias: Oh son of heaven!
Empedocles: I was the one! yes! and want now to tell it.

TEXTUAL REFERENCE

Halbgötter denk' ich jetzt
Und kennen muß ich die Theuern,
Weil oft ihr Leben so
Die sehnende Brust mir beweget.
Wem aber, wie, Rousseau, dir,
Unüberwindlich die Seele
Die starkausdauernde ward,
Und sicherer Sinn
Und die süße Gaabe zu hören,
Zu reden so, daß er aus heiliger Fülle
Wie der Weingott, thörig göttlich
Und gesezlos sie die Sprache der Reinesten giebt
Verständlich den Guten, aber mit Recht
Die Achtungslosen mit Blindheit schlägt
Die entweihenden Knechte, wie nenn ich den Fremden?

Die Söhne der Erde sind, wie die Mutter,
Allliebend, so empfangen sie auch
Mühlos, die Glücklichen, Alles.
Drum überraschet es auch
Und schröckt den sterblichen Mann,
Wenn er den Himmel, den
Er mit den liebenden Armen
Sich auf die Schultern gehäufft,
Und die Last der Freude bedenket;
Dann scheint ihm oft das Beste,
Fast ganz vergessen da,
Wo der Stral nicht brennt,
Im Schatten des Walds
Am Bielersee in frischer Grüne zu seyn,
Und sorglosarm an Tönen,
Anfängern gleich, bei Nachtigallen zu lernen.

Und herrlich ists, aus heiligem Schlafe dann
Erstehen und aus Waldes Kühle
Erwachend, Abends nun
Dem milderen Licht entgegenzugehn,
Wenn, der die Berge gebaut
Und den Pfad der Ströme gezeichnet,
Nachdem er lächelnd auch
Der Menschen geschäftiges Leben
Das othemarme, wie Seegel
Mit seinen Lüften gelenkt hat,
Auch ruht und zu der Schülerin jezt,
Der Bildner, Gutes mehr
Denn Böses findend,
Zur heutigen Erde der Tag sich neiget.
—(*Sämtliche Werke* 2, 146f.)

Of demigods now I think
And I must know these dear ones
Because so often their lives
Move me and fill me with longing.
But he whose soul, like yours,
Rousseau, ever strong and patient,
Became invincible,

Endowed with steadfast purpose
And a sweet gift of hearing,
Of speaking, so that from holy profusion
Like the wine-god foolishly, divinely
And lawlessly he gives it away,
The language of the purest, comprehensible to the good,
But rightly strikes with blindness the irreverent,
The profaning rabble, what shall I call that stranger?

   The sons of Earth, like their mother, are
All-loving, so without effort too
All things those blessed ones receive.
And therefore it surprises
And startles the mortal man
When he considers the heaven
Which with loving arms he himself
Has heaped upon his shoulders,
And feels the burden of joy;
Then often to him it seems best
Almost wholly forgotten to be
Where the beam does not sear,
In the forest's shade
By Lake Bienne amid foliage newly green,
And blithely poor in tones,
Like beginners, to learn from nightingales.

   And glorious then it is to arise once more
From holy sleep and awakening
From coolness of the woods, at evening
Walk now toward the softer light
When he who built the mountains
And drafted the paths of the rivers,
Having also smiling directed
The busy lives of men,
So short of breath, like sails,
And filled them with his breezes,
Reposes also, and down to his pupil
The master craftsmen, finding
More good than evil,
Day now inclines to the present Earth.

In Hölderlin's Rhine hymn we encounter the name Rousseau. The mention of Lake Bienne makes the reference less general than, for instance, in the ode titled *Rousseau*, where clear references to specific works are lacking. In the Rhine hymn, Hölderlin evokes the fifth promenade from the *Rêveries du promeneur solitaire* (Reveries of the solitary walker), where Rousseau tells of his stay on St. Peter's Island. Since one text refers to another, we might ask what kind of relationship exists between the two. Every previous attempt to illuminate the role of Rousseau in Hölderlin's poem answers our question without really considering what happens when one text refers to another. In this particular case it is important to note that these references belong to a later draft of the poem, both "Rousseau" and "Lake Bienne" being penciled in the manuscript (2, 727). This raises questions about the reference to Rousseau. On the one hand it seems to complete the last step of the poem, that is, it adds the last missing part. On the other hand it seems to be nothing more than a simple supplement that provides another illustration of what was already there. Accordingly the name Rousseau is either essential or superfluous. All interpretations expressly or implicitly represent one or the other view.

If the name, as an afterthought, stands for something already present, then the attempt to create a bridge between Hölderlin's and Rousseau's text is pointless, since whatever the name Rousseau brings to the text could have been gleaned from the poem itself. Heidegger comments on the Rhine hymn, remarking that the reference to Rousseau's name is a later addition: "The original interpretation of the stanza must therefore be kept free of any reference to Rousseau, only the sense of the entire stanza can explain why the poet here is also able to name Rousseau" (*Oeuvres complètes* 39, 278). To the extent that Rousseau "is also able" to name Rousseau, the reference becomes unnecessary. Since nothing would be lost by its absence, it is superfluous and could be deleted without compromising the comprehension of the text. This consequence, not articulated in Heidegger's text, raises questions about the attempt to connect Rousseau to the poem based solely on context. Doing so preserves both the poem's self-sufficiency and the reader's ability to understand it in and of itself, but the foreign name becomes superfluous in that it is explained within the poem's context. Since it cannot be integrated, it becomes a nuisance that cannot be ignored. The difficulties are no less if the reference to Rousseau is taken to be a necessary addition to the poem as a whole. The reference does not realize itself but opens itself to the foreign text, thereby questioning its own self-sufficiency. But since the reference to the foreign text is assumed to be necessary, the poem's integrity can no longer be preserved by ignoring it. It must be reestablished via a discussion of Rousseau. Such a discussion must enable us to see the names "Rousseau" and "Lake Bienne" so that what is named in them can be meaningfully incorporated into the context of the poem. Any interpretation that attempts to do this aspires to ascertain Hölderlin's view of Rousseau. This is based on the premise that the name Rousseau means something in particular to Hölderlin and that this meaning is incorporated in the Rhine hymn. If we can succeed in reconstructing Hölderlin's interpretation of Rousseau's text, then we can substitute this reconstruction for the name in the poem. If, however, the poem is an interpretation and in turn an appropriation of the foreign text, then the reference becomes superfluous again, because, as an appropriation, it is no longer foreign but integral to Hölderlin's poem, which then replaces it. The integrity of the poem is regained via the foreign by reducing it to its own. It remains incomprehensible why Rousseau is named at all. As an appropriation, he is no longer in need of a name.

In the appropriation of the foreign as well as in its suppression, one senses the refusal to deal with it because it is unsettling. The foreign is unsettling insofar as the foreign cannot be integrated. By referring to the foreign text, the poem admits to being dependent on it and thereby questions its own integrity. The text that opens itself to the foreign and refuses to appropriate it saves itself from the interpreter's appropriation. All inclination to put aside the foreign as foreign is due to the drive to regain the text's domination, something Hölderlin refuses. It would be premature to justify the rejection of such attempts with the notion that the poem speaks of the foreign. The fact that the foreign is discussed, as in "what shall I call that stranger?" and the assertions that accompany these references make the preservation of the poem's integrity possible. The poem by no means delivers itself up to the foreign simply by mentioning it. Rather, the stranger is available as something named and can be integrated into the whole. This is why Heidegger attempts to read the text with reference to the "foreign" and not to "Rousseau." Insofar as Rousseau can be identified as the stranger, he is already integrated into Hölderlin's poem. "The stranger" is not the presence of the foreign as such in the poem but rather its linguistic subjugation. This changes if Rousseau is no longer called "the stranger" but the foreigner is called "Rousseau." As "Rousseau," Rousseau *is* the foreigner, something he is only *named* as "the stranger." The foreign is recognized as foreign in a name. It realizes the foreignness that is only expressed in the word "the stranger." To the extent that the names "Rousseau" and "Lake Bienne" remain expressionless, and as long as they don't speak based on information that can only be gained from outside the poem, the foreign remains present in the poem. The name as the foreign is the name of the foreign in the name "Rousseau." This can explain the later addition of the name in the manuscript as Hölderlin's answer to the question: what shall I call that stranger? The stranger is named with the name, not in a way that makes him familiar or no longer foreign. The stranger is addressed in the otherness of his irreducible individuality. The stranger is not in the name, because the word "stranger" is understood as a foreigner, already subdued and appropriated. The name may hit at the heart of whomever owns it, but since the heart of the other remains distant, the name is incomprehensible. It names the most personal of the other in its foreignness.

The individuality of the foreigner named Rousseau is to a certain extent restricted. The phrase "but he whose soul, like yours, Rousseau" (v. 139) states that everything that the stanza lists holds true for Rousseau, but also for whomever is like Rousseau. Those who are like Rousseau can only exist if some commonality binds them together, in which case they are not foreign. Whatever Rousseau has in common with others, be it only a potential, is not what makes him a foreigner. It is what is understood about him that makes it possible for others to appropriate him. And still we want to read the phrase so that the listed characteristics make Rousseau and those like him become foreigners. The problem can be solved if we recognize that the foreignness is viewed on a new level. Foreign is what is outside the text and what cannot be reduced to the text, the other text. Foreign can also be what is within the text, figures estranged from their surroundings, with long-lived souls and the gift of hearing and speech, such as the poets in *Hyperion*: "Die Guten! Sie leben in der Welt, wie Fremdlinge im eigenen Hauße, sie sind so recht, wie der Dulder Ulyß, da er in Bettlers-gestalt an seiner Thüre saß, indeß die unverschämten Freier im Saale lärmten und fragten, wer hat uns den Landläufer gebracht?" (These good souls! They live in the world like strangers in their own house, they are like Ulysses, the enduring, as he sat at his own doorstep while the brazen suitors reveled in the hall and asked, who brought us this vagabond? [3, 155]). Here the foreign element is no longer what is accessible to discourse but what is expressed by it. Insofar as we can talk about the foreigner, he is no longer a foreigner but a relative accessible in his likeness.

The double meaning of foreignness bridges the gap between foreignness and appropriation in the reference of Hölderlin's poem to Rousseau. This tension should not be ignored while attempting to demonstrate the relationship between the two texts. Whereas the appropriation has received plenty of attention, the foreignness has gone unnoticed, even though the addition of the proper names "Rousseau" and "Lake Bienne" is Hölderlin's express reference to the nonappropriated and the nonappropriatable. The requisite recourse to a text of Rousseau is only defensible to the extent that a complete appropriation does not take place, because this would replace the foreign text and make it untenable. Because this re-placement does not take place, and the reference to the foreign text allows it to continue to exist, Rousseau remains the foreigner, and his text remains unvanquished. The relationship between Hölder-lin and Rousseau cannot be defined and remains open. Hölderlin's notion of Rousseau can only tendentiously exist in this openness. It remains incomplete as long as the text and its relationship to the other text stays open-ended.

The open-ended relationship between the two texts is the conversation between them. It lasts as long as one does not appropriate and overwhelm the other. In that Hölderlin's poem allows Rousseau's text to remain foreign, it does not read it by force. The open-ended conversation is never-ending, and the reader is invited to join in. The relationship between the two texts is thus never defined and must always be established anew. It would therefore be unproductive to want to reconstruct Hölderlin's view of Rousseau—not, however, to construct it. This is the task of the reader, who must become productive to the extent that the texts are open-ended. In the Rhine hymn, the reference to the foreign text invokes the reader's text as a third, the reader being responsible for constructing the dialogue between the other two. It is necessary to continue this conversation because Hölderlin starts it without finishing it. As long as the conversation remains open-ended, it cannot be replaced by affirmative statements. The assumption that it could solidify into hard and fast assertions contradicts the openness of the text, which only exists as long as the conversation continues. Every statement remains subject to foreign objections and thereby to its own doubt. But keeping the text open-ended is not sufficient reason alone to keep the dialogue between Hölderlin and Rousseau going. The text is open-ended precisely because the conversation is unfinished, that is, it breaks off. If it is taken up again, then the hope is raised that some result might be achieved. Wanting to revert to Rousseau's text is in part motivated by the attempt to appropriate it in the name of Hölderlin, even though this would disregard Hölderlin's recognition of the foreignness in the other. For both tendencies to coexist, the reading of the text itself, as the continuation of the conversation, must take place suspended between foreignness and appropriation, the place Hölderlin's poem occupies. Without this tension, there is no conversation.

If the reader is to assume the responsibility of constructing the conversation between texts, then it remains unclear how this can be done. Texts that converse are not subject to any specific hierarchy.

This could be inferred from the chronology that makes Hölderlin's reference to Rousseau possible but does not seem to allow for the reverse. Either way, the one or the other text could be privileged based on this sequence, but only if we want to see texts as something unalterably present and available only once and for all. Hölderlin's reference to Rousseau, insofar as it is not only appropriation, rehabilitates the unavailability of the text by recognizing its foreignness. In that the texts continue to speak as something read, they change. Rousseau's text is not what it was before Hölderlin's poem. It is not enough to read Hölderlin via Rousseau, as if we knew what Rousseau was. We must instead read Rousseau via Hölderlin to let him become the one who actually had an effect on Hölderlin. In doing so we must always consider that Hölderlin does not say what Rousseau is, since it would then seem unnecessary to read his texts, at least as far as Hölderlin's poem is concerned. But the Rhine hymn does provide clues that could be construed as guidelines for a discussion of Rousseau. What is gained by following them is not Hölderlin's interpretation of Rousseau's text but rather an independent interpretation based on Hölderlin's suggestions, measured by its contribution to the understanding of Hölderlin's poem. The relationship between Hölderlin and Rousseau so constructed is a game between two teams that spur each other on. It is not a definitive result but a point in the conversation between the texts.

We might ask in what direction the clues in Hölderlin's poem point. The mention of Lake Bienne has caused those interpreters interested in the relationship with Rousseau to assume that Hölderlin is primarily interested in the experiences Rousseau relates in the Fifth Walk concerning his stay on St. Peter's Island. This track has been supported by the fact that recent literature on Rousseau has taken a similar course, seeking mainly to understand the dreamer's frame of mind as well as Rousseau's existential feeling described in the Fifth Walk. Although this aspect of Rousseau's text is certainly not unimportant for Hölderlin, and his Rousseau's desire to be on Lake Bienne can hardly be directed at anything else, the exclusivity with which Rousseau's meaning for Hölderlin has been sought in this aspect of Rousseau's text rests on a rather inexact reading of Hölderlin's formulations. Important is not only what Rousseau experienced on Lake Bienne.

> Dann scheint ihm oft das Beste,
> Fast ganz vergessen da,
> Wo der Stral nicht brennt,
> Im Schatten des Walds
> Am Bielersee in frischer Grüne zu seyn,
> Und sorglosarm an Tönen,
> Anfängern gleich, bei Nachtigallen zu lernen.

> Then often to him it seems best
> Almost wholly forgotten to be
> Where the beam does not sear,
> In the forest's shade
> By Lake Bienne amid foliage newly green,
> And blithely poor in tones,
> Like beginners, to learn from nightingales.

"Then often to him it seems best": this is not about the one who is at Lake Bienne but the one for whom being there seems the best. Not only the related experiences, but above all their being told, are important. It is therefore wrong simply to want to insert in the Rhine hymn a dreaming Rousseau on the lake shore, however one might interpret the dreamer's frame of mind. Hölderlin's Rousseau is not on St. Peter's but rather in a situation that can be more precisely determined in the context of the poem, where he looks back on his stay as the best. Rousseau is not only the character in the Fifth Walk, but also the one who writes. Hölderlin reads this text not just as information. He is interested in the relationship between the narrator and the narrated. Rousseau, not as someone presently experiencing but as someone who remembers past experiences, is the contemplative introduced as:

> Drum überraschet es auch
> Und schrökt den sterblichen Mann,
> Wenn er den Himmel, den

Er mit den liebenden Armen
Sich auf die Schultern gehäufft,
Und die Last der Freude bedenket;

And therefore it surprises
And startles the mortal man
When he considers the heaven
Which with loving arms he himself
Has heaped upon his shoulders,
And feels the burden of joy;

The Fifth Walk was created out of this consideration, if we take the *Dann* in v. 159 seriously, and this discourse concerns Hölderlin above all in what it bespeaks. It is pointless to try to establish links to the content of Rousseau's text; they are almost entirely missing. The amazing thing about Hölderlin's reference to Rousseau lies in the fact that there are no apparent similarities. Rousseau does not appear in Hölderlin's text in what he says but always and expressly as the speaker. We learn that he articulates the language of the purest and learns from nightingales, but we do not discover what he says and signs. The insight, supported by the wording of the Rhine hymn, that Hölderlin is concerned not only with what is expressed in Rousseau's text but primarily with its expression, tends to reorient a Hölderlin-related reading of the Fifth Walk. The shift away from what is expressed to the act of speaking is the most important guidance that can be gleaned from Hölderlin's poem. Following this guidance leads to a focus not on the same worn-out old passages but on neglected passages that speak of the relationship between the narrator and the narrative and what is narrated. The Fifth Walk was created out of this consideration, if we take the predicted with as little certainty as can its effects on the understanding of the Rousseau passage in the Rhine hymn.

ROUSSEAU'S FIFTH WALK

The simply constructed Fifth Walk is divided into two main parts, the first of which (pars. 1–11) is more of a narrative, the second (pars. 12–17) more of a reflective nature. The first part can again be divided. In an introduction (1–6), Rousseau describes St. Peter's (1–3), tells of the circumstances of his stay there (4–5), and asks wherein the happiness lies that he has found there (6). Looking ahead to an answer to this question, the second half of the first part (7–11) describes the daily routine on the island, and finally (11), the question, in what way this life has become a happy one, is repeated. In the second part (12–17), the question is answered in an explanation of the nature of *rêverie*. After the emphasis on the importance and difficulty of lasting happiness (12–13), *rêverie* is shown to be one possible realization of such a happiness (14–16). In the closing passage (17), Rousseau evokes once again his frame of mind on the island and tries to understand his relationship to it is as one who remembers.

The organization shows that the text is more than just a characterization of *rêverie* as an existential feeling, which some of his readers have restricted it to. Two ways of relating to what is said are examined in narration and explanation, and at the end the relationship between the one who remembers and the remembered, on the one hand, and the experience of remembering, on the other, is, compared to the remembered experience in the text, a theme in itself. The attempt to read the text with Hölderlin's guidelines in mind, the importance of how Rousseau as speaker stands to what he says, is justified by Rousseau's text, because it is not only concerned with *rêverie* but also with its placement vis-à-vis the discourse that bespeaks it. Instead of viewing this existential feeling in isolation, we have to try to understand its place in the whole of the text, because only in this way does the meaning of its being expressed become accessible.

Existential feeling and the circumstances under which it occurs are described in paragraph 9.

> As evening approached, I came down from the heights of the island, and I liked then to go and sit on the shingle in some secluded spot by the edge of the lake; there the noise of the lake and the movement of the water, taking hold of my senses and driving all other agitation from

my soul, would plunge it into a delicious reverie in which night often stole upon me unawares. The ebb and flow of the water, its continuous yet undulating noise, kept lapping against my ears and my eyes, taking the place of all the inward movements which my reverie had calmed within me, and it was enough to make me pleasurably aware of my existence, without troubling myself with thought. From time to time some brief and insubstantial reflection arose concerning the instability of the things of this world, whose image I saw in the surface of the water, but soon these fragile impressions gave way before the unchanging and ceaseless movement which lulled me and without any active effort on my part occupied me so completely that even when time and the habitual signal called me home I could hardly bring myself to go. (*Oeuvres complètes* I, 1045)

What is happening here should not be misunderstood as shutting out the environment and withdrawing to some inner self. The soul may quiet itself, not because the environment no longer exists, but because the environment is of such a nature that it quiets all unrest. The senses are not suppressed but fixed on the external movement ("the movement of the water") that replaces internal unrest ("all other agitation"). The internal unrest that must be eliminated, because it would otherwise obstruct access to related experiences, is passion ("But most men being continually agitated by passions know little of this condition" [1047]). Passion disrupts the cooperation between internal and external. The movement that displaces all internal movement is the back and forth of the waves ("the ebb and flow of the water"). This movement makes sufficient demands to prevent any sense of deficiency from cropping up and keeps the senses occupied but is never sensed so strongly that thinking would need to overcome it. The external is cradling and carrying, and the internal conforms to this rhythm. All objective sense is lost, and all that is left is the pure feeling of being in the world. This existential feeling of being carried through one's surroundings can only come about if the external is experienced not as object but as sojourn. This most likely succeeds where, as on an island surrounded by water, the surroundings are only present in that they surround. This being surrounded is buried underneath overriding change just as it crumbles in the wasteland of complete stagnation. If the environment is unnoticeable enough to be forgotten yet noticeable enough to be remembered, then it allows whomever it encompasses to experience the perfect harmony of being carried and of carrying.

The back and forth of the waves is able to effect this equilibrium between internal and external, provided the soul yields to the soothing evenness of its rhythm as the existential feeling is suspended. But the motion of the waves can only invoke the experience of equilibrium of internal and external in the observer because it is itself already an image of this equilibrium. The external favors most the balance between internal and external, which is in itself balanced. And so the equilibrium is not restricted to the back and forth of the waves but epitomizes for Rousseau the entire Lake Bienne landscape, which makes the experience of the environment as a nondisruptive carrier possible. The importance of the environment's internal harmony is most apparent when it is disrupted. In his description of the lake, Rousseau mentions a second, smaller, and uninhabited island. It is said that it will eventually disappear because all its earth is being transported to the larger island to repair storm and wave damage. "Thus it is that the substance of the weak always goes to profit the powerful" (1041). The mention of this small island is connected with the power vacuum between large and small, which destroys equilibrium (1044). When Rousseau, with the ceremonious participation of the local inhabitants, takes a litter of rabbits to the small island and lets them go, the founding of this colony is to be seen as an attempt to save an endangered equilibrium. The ceremonial crossing represents the back and forth of the dirt transports, which reduce the substance of the island.

The condition of the balanced exchange between internal and external, created by the surrounding nature and at the same time represented in it, can be regarded as the message Rousseau's text attempts to transmit. This transmission transpires on the one hand as narration, on the other hand as explanation, and we must question the purpose of this dual approach. As for the narrative, the text indicates that it fulfills the purpose of the remembered realization. After the description of the island's typical daily routine, we read: "even fifteen years later I am incapable of thinking of this cherished spot without each time being transported by pangs of longing" (1045). And at the end Rousseau preserves the prospect of remembering his stay on the island against those who drove him from his refuge on St. Peter's: "But at least they will not prevent me from transporting myself daily on the wings of imagination and from tasting for several hours the same pleasure as if I were still living there" (1049). The narration aims at reliving past experience. In the realization of the past, the distance to it is overcome, and the lost is reestablished. The narration facilitates an inebriation by means of what is narrated, enabling its language to be forgotten and what is experienced to be rediscovered.

Why do we need to explain the narration? Rousseau himself offers an explanation for the explanation. The narration is provoked by the question of the nature of happiness on the island. "What then was this happiness and wherein lay this great contentment? The men of this age would never guess the answer from a description of the life I led there" (1042). The challenge of explaining happiness based on the narration is repeated at the end of the narration: "I should like to know what there was in it that was attractive enough to give me such deep, tender and lasting regrets that even fifteen years later . . . " (1045). It should, in Rousseau's view, be self-evident that life as it is described is happiness. But it is so uneventful and quiet that his contemporaries ("men of this age"), who seek happiness in the unusual, in the "brief moments of madness and passion" (1046), have no appreciation for it. "But most men being continually stirred by passion know little of this condition, and having enjoyed it only fleetingly and incompletely they retain no more than a dim and confused notion of it and are unaware of its true charm" (1047). Because these people fail to see that and how this life is a happy one, they need an explanation. This justification is unsatisfying to the extent that it is based not on the narrative as something to be explained but on the failings of certain readers.

If the need for explanation springs from the narrative itself, then the narrative only makes what is to be told partially accessible and requires the help of another discourse. The explanation is necessary to the extent that something is missing in the narrative. If we assume that the narrative makes what is told present in a way that allows the experience to be repeated, as Rousseau tells himself, then the fault lies not with the narrative, which delivers all that is expected of it, but with the experience that is retold. But the nature of island life is again and again described as one of complete happiness and lacking nothing: "I look upon these months as the happiest time of my life, so happy that I would have been content to live all my life in this way, without a moment's desire for any other state" (1042). The description of happiness in the second part leaves no doubt as to the perfection of this state.

> But if there is a state where the soul can find a resting place secure enough to establish itself and concentrate its entire being there, with no need to remember the past or reach into the future, where time is nothing to it, where the present runs on indefinitely but this duration goes unnoticed, with no sign of the passing of time, and no other feeling of deprivation or enjoyment, pleasure or pain, desire or fear than the simple feeling of existence, a feeling that fills our soul entirely, as long as this state lasts, we can call ourselves happy, not with a poor, incomplete and relative happiness such as we find in the pleasures of life, but with a sufficient, complete and perfect happiness which leaves no emptiness to be filled in the soul. Such is the state I often experienced on St. Peter's Island in my solitary reveries, whether I lay in a boat and drifted where the water carried me, or sat by the shores of the stormy lake, or elsewhere, on the banks of a lovely river or a stream murmuring over the stones. (1046f.)

This characterization of Rousseau's happy state of mind practically demands a comparison with divine self-sufficiency: "as long as this state lasts we are self-sufficient like God" (1047). How can any explanation be added to this perfect wealth and then be understood as a supplement to something that seems to need no augmentation? This wealth has the fault that it is has no fault to make its perfection discernible. In this wealth's lack of contrast, the ability to recognize its completeness is lost. This only becomes appreciable— or, to use Hölderlin's word, perceivable—when it no longer exists and becomes determinable based on a regained incompleteness as its opposite. In Rousseau's text, the explanation comes from a distance the narration tries to overcome. The narration, even if, especially if, it were to succeed in reestablishing the divine self-sufficiency of happiness through the evocation of island life, could never say this in its perfection, whereas the explanation achieves this by its exclusion from this happiness. The blindness of happiness towards itself is its speechlessness. It disappears in being expressed. Insofar as both the narration and the explanation are ways of expression, the difference between the two is not easily maintained. Perfection is lost even in narration if it can be expressed. Narration strives to overcome its own being in language through the total realization of what is narrated. Explanation remains at arm's length to understand it instead of succumbing to the illusion of its reality. The difference between the tendency of both manners of discourse justifiably remains and allows us to see the strange position of the explanation better. This offers us an understanding of happiness that happiness lacks. Since happiness is the absence of shortcomings, one who is happy does not perceive the lack of understanding to be an imperfection. This only comes into play retrospectively, when it is corrected by the explanation. The explanation bestows this shortcoming on the perfect self-sufficiency of happiness and then constitutes itself as its elimination. Insofar as it adds something that was not previously present, the explanation is necessary. Insofar as what it adds is perfect and complete, it becomes superfluous. It is paradoxically a necessary excess. The second, explanatory part of the Fifth Walk is thus to be incorporated in the entire text, even though it cannot be included. It is an augmentation that comes to the narrative and complements it, even though it should actually be self-sufficient and is not recognizably deficient until it is supplemented.

Narration, as opposed to explanation, is understood as the refer-

ential realization of what is narrated, the complement to perfection
that must be considered superfluous and necessary at the same
time, because it is an augmentation to something that does not
leave room for it and yet still is incomplete. It can be shown that
not only the explanation behaves in this manner towards the
narrative but also the narration to what is narrated. This can be
demonstrated in an exact reading of the final section of the Fifth
Walk. This section is divided in three parts. In the first, Rousseau
thinks back once more to his stay on Lake Bienne and to the
dreamlike life he led. In the nostalgic middle section, he regrets
that he cannot return to St. Peter's and the lifestyle he enjoyed
there. The third section expresses that, despite the impossibility of
returning, no one can stop him from reliving the past happiness in
his imagination.

The third section illustrates the situation of one who remembers
the lost past and in dreaming relives the narrator's situation. His
relationship to the narrative is outlined in a few sentences:

> But at least they will not prevent me from transporting myself daily on
> the wings of imagination and from tasting for several hours the same
> pleasure as if I were still living there. Were I there, my sweetest
> occupation would be to dream to my heart's content. Is it not the same
> thing to dream that I am there? Better still, I can add to my abstract
> and monotonous reveries charming images that give them life. During
> my moments of ecstasy the sources of these images often escaped my
> senses; but now the deeper the reverie, the more vividly they are
> present to me. I am often more truly in their midst, and they give me
> still greater pleasure than when I was surrounded by them. (1049)

The situation of remembering and the remembered situation have
one thing in common: dreaming. Rousseau tended to dream on the
island but now dreams of being on the island. These two kinds of
dreaming are at first equated, even if only in a question: "Is it not
the same thing to dream that I am there?" A differentiation follows.
Dreaming *on* the island appears as "abstract and monotonous
reveries." The deprecating tone of this characterization is surprising, if we consider that we are discussing the faultless condition of

divine self-sufficiency, something that has just been celebrated. The fact that this reevaluation is at first unexplained does not diminish the contrast to the dreaming *of* the island, which is ranked higher because it produces images. This differentiation between pictorial and nonpictorial dreaming already appears in the second-to-last section of the text (1047f.). Rousseau's dreaming on the island was nonpictorial. This imageless dreaming is bound to certain environmental conditions described in the narrative part of the Fifth Walk and generally mentioned in the explanatory part. The environment must be perceivable just enough so that it is sensed neither as defect nor as intrusion. If it is too demanding, there is no dreaming, because the external pulls the soul away from itself and occupies it. Dreaming is possible if the environment is lifeless, for example, in prison, because then the imagination of what is missing externally can always be replaced. "The movement that does not come from outside us arises within us at such times" (1048). This dreaming is no longer imageless, as if internal and external were balanced, but rather pictorial to the extent that the imperfection of the environment is compensated for by the imagined images.

The separation of nonpictorial and pictorial dreaming seems at first to be easily transferred to the entire text. The ideal conditions were present at Lake Bienne, and nonpictorial dreaming was possible. For the narrator looking back, these conditions are no longer present, and he must call on his imagination to regain them as things represented. But the text cannot be read in such a simplistic manner, first because the images not only supplement what is missing, and second because the dreaming on the island, as it is described at the beginning of the last section, is unexpectedly pictorial.

The one who looks back places himself in a dreamlike state that he remembers as past. He dreams that he dreams on the island. The recovery of the past experience requires referential illusion, in which the language of the remembered, which is in this case the dreaminess of the dream, is forgotten, just as the narrative is taken to be the thing itself in the narrative part of the Fifth Walk. The role of images in this recollective dreaming should then consist of creating the conditions for nonpictorial dreaming, which are no longer present through the representation of the past environment. The images would have to disappear to exactly the same extent to which they appear, because imageless dreaming demands an environment no longer experienced in its presence but felt as a supporting structure. Rousseau's text, however, does not allow us to conclude that the environment of the remembered island landscape, reproduced in images, disappears in its pictorialization by freeing the soul for the earlier, nonpictorial dreaming. It is expressly emphasized that the appeal of the earlier dreaming was increased in its repetition when objects that were at first not experienced are added to the experience. This is why dreaming *of* the island cannot be equated with dreaming *on* the island, but is more: "In dreaming that I am there, am I not doing the same thing? I do even more; I add charming pictures that vivify the abstract and monotonous reverie" (1049). Since the condition of nonpictorial dreaming, based on its description throughout the text, is thought to be perfect bliss, the images of the recollective dreaming become an addition to what is already complete. The excess is an augmentation of the whole. Rousseau does not recognize excessive augmentation as such but prefers to accept a contradiction by denouncing nonpictorial dreaming as "abstract and monotonous reverie." Its deficiency is made good by images that can be integrated into a whole that would otherwise be incomplete without them. Regardless of whether the augmentation is added as excess to the whole or as supplement to the imperfect, we are left with the curious conclusion that what is remembered in remembering is more than it was in reality. Contrary to first impressions, the relationship between the remembering narrator and the narrative in the Fifth Walk is not nostalgic. The narrative is superior to what was experienced. Narration is a superior experience to what is narrated. The narration, as a representation of what was, is not a makeshift substitute but an escalation. The linguistic rendering of what was is more than what was.

Pictorial dreaming and the problem of incorporating it into the whole of the text already present themselves at the beginning of the final section. Rousseau seems at first to want to recall the previously detailed description of island life. After considering ways to experience the joys of dreaming in the previous section, under even less fortuitous circumstances, the beginning of the last section sketches the ideal conditions for the dreamer on St. Peter's. It says that the company of the inhabitants of the island was "attractive and pleasing without being so interesting as to constantly occupy me" (1048) and that the guest was able to follow his interests "without care or hindrance." The surroundings correspond to previous descriptions and are defined in that they allow neither too little nor too much. The relationship to the environment is so balanced that any demands it makes are not perceived as such. Although such a relationship with nature was earlier seen as a precondition for imageless dreaming, the dreams that Rousseau claims to have had on St. Peter's are now characterized by their pictorial nature.

> It was without doubt a fine opportunity for a dreamer who is capable of enjoying the most delightful fantasies even in the most unpleasant settings, and who could here feed on them at leisure, enriching them with all the objects that his senses actually perceived. Emerging from a long and happy reverie, seeing myself surrounded by greenery, flowers, and birds, and letting my eyes wander over the picturesque far-off shores, which enclosed a vast stretch of clear and crystalline water, I fused my imaginings with these charming sights, and finding myself in the end gradually brought back to myself and my surroundings, I could not draw a line between fiction and reality; so much did everything conspire equally to make me love the contemplative and solitary life I led in that beautiful place. (1048)

What appear here as "agréables chimères" and "fictions" are images created by the imagination that really have no place in the perfection Rousseau experiences. This is made clear if we question the relationship of the images (*fictions*) to what is really present (*réalités*). It is characterized at first by the verb *concourir*, which appears twice, expressing that reality is shaped in such a way that it contributes to the dream and at the same time can be included in it.

The dream image (*chimère*) and what encounters the senses in the outside world ("ce qui frappot reellement ses sens") are so closely connected that neither can be differentiated. This is demonstrated in awakening, something described as the transition from dream to reality but also as a state where changes no longer take place, because dream and reality are the same, and the borders between the two do not exist: "I could not draw a line between fiction and reality." If, however, what is dreamed is already present in reality, then the dream becomes superfluous, because it is added to reality when reality has no need for addition.

The introduction of the unnecessary pictorial dream makes it difficult, maybe even impossible, to incorporate the final section into the context of the entire text. The assumption that the narration is summarized and retold after the interpretive remarks of paragraphs 12–16 is untenable. Something completely new is reported that does not correspond to the previous narration. It is even more difficult to join the final paragraph (17) to the explanatory section. After it has been remarked under what conditions imagination must become active to make dreaming possible, images are created where they are not needed. In that the pictorial dream takes place under conditions previously associated only with nonpictorial dreaming, the argument falls apart. The beginning of the final paragraph cannot be incorporated into the order of the entire preceding text. It is conversely not difficult to recognize a kinship between the first and third parts of the final paragraph. This correspondence is based on the richness of the image, which does not represent something missing but is added to a complete whole. This similarity of the two text parts is made more interesting in that the one is concerned with recollective narration and the other with recalled narrative. Based on this, we can reconstruct the relationship between the narration and the narrative. The examination of the situation of the narration has demonstrated that dreaming *of* the island is more than dreaming *on* the island, because images are added to objects that were not perceived at the time. This augmentation of the images is now carried over from the situation of the narration to the narrated situation. The first part of the final paragraph tells of the past as if the augmentation of the images, only realized in the recollective retrospective, were already present. It is told as if the present objects had already been represented, that is, dreamed. What is not present until the level of the narration is asserted for the narrative's level. In this way the narration contradicts itself. The situation of the narration reaches into the narrative and destroys its coherence. The narration at the beginning of the last paragraph is wrenched from the context of what is reported, where it seems out of place. It does not allow itself to be incorporated into the order of the narrative and is only comprehensible, as it is presented in the third part of the final paragraph, from the perspective of the narration.

The transfer of the "augmentation of images" from narration to the narrative is an attempt to come to grips with the paradoxical fact that the narrative is complete and the narration is more than just the narrative. It would be more correct to say that the narrative is more than the experience and that the experience is poetically enhanced as something it can only be as narrative. By attributing the augmentation to the experience, Rousseau tries to overcome the gap that separates the narrative from the experience. The scandal of the superfluous remains, only now it has taken effect in the experience, thereby becoming the already narrated. This excessive augmentation is at best representation. In the recollective dreaming of the past, the representation of the real environment is the supplement to the remembered nonpictorial dream. In the subsequent attempt to integrate this augmentation with the recalled dreaming on St. Peter's, the dream becomes the double representation of reality and therefore superfluous, because everything is already present without it.

The problem of narration of the Fifth Walk is the representation of perfection. The problem lies in the fact that Rousseau situates perfection first, where representation no longer exists, and where the unmediated presence of the thing itself is dominant. Perfection is therefore nonlinguistic, and its nonexistence in language can be taken two ways. If it is perfect to be nonlinguistic, then language is a fault that must be overcome to reach perfection. But if language, as the manifestation of perfection, is not a fault, then the absence of language is the fault of perfection, and only language can make it what it is. Both are true: perfection's absence of language allows it to be direct and is also its fault, that is, the impossibility to manifest itself as perfect. In the mediation that included it, perfection is lost. Language, subjected to perfection, is the necessary but superfluous excess. It is excessive because it is added to the nonlinguistic perfection that survives without it. It loses itself in that it must conceal its characteristic directness to be able to appear to itself.

THE BEST AND THE HIGHEST

The section of the Rhine hymn dedicated to Rousseau is divided into the three initially quoted stanzas (10–12). Rousseau is at first the speaker who imparts the language of the purest. He does not impart content but language. Nowhere do we read what is said, but we read everywhere about the way things are spoken. The "foolish, divine, and lawless" manner of speech is that of one inspired, through which more is said than what he himself is. Out of his own limitations, he is placed not in a contralegal but in a prelegal condition, standing open to the divine and passing it on without realizing what he is doing. The speaker is not master of the language he speaks. He may present it but only as the gift given him, the language of the purest. This gift is not received without merit. It "became" to him just as the persevering soul became unconquerable. The perseverance in which the soul became un-conquerable is the persistence in hearing's receptivity, connected to a speaking where the speaker breaks through to something greater. In the following stanza, the discourse of the one given over to hearing the divine is interrupted. Thoughtfulness takes the place of effortless reception. This is a pause on the straight path of dis-course. In contemplation, the received is recognized as a burden, and being startled by the burden of heaven leads to fear. The self-lessness of the speaker in the tenth stanza gives way in the eleventh to the realization of the disproportionate nature of burden and carrier. It is from this perspective of the disproportion between heaven and mortal humans that we are to read the second part of the stanza as Rousseau's answer to the fear in reflection. However we might understand the reference to the Fifth Walk, it leads in any case to a more balanced and less dangerous relationship to the divine, in the twelfth stanza no longer a foreboding burning stream of light but an inviting "softer light."

The question that is now raised concerns the relationship of these three stanzas to Rousseau's Fifth Walk, as I have attempted to read it based on the guidelines in Hölderlin's poem. This should not raise the expectation that everything that is said about Rousseau can or should be related to his text. The theme of the entire passage is the relationship between man and the divine and especially the danger of the divine for those subjected to it. This Hölderlinian theme that dominates the preceding passage (sts. 7–9) does not come from Rousseau. Hölderlin apparently has found in Rousseau a certain, obviously exemplary, way of relating the connection to the divine. The Fifth Walk is mentioned just when the sudden realization of the weight of divine power gives way to fear. Rousseau's text represents the conquering of this fear and the potential of a supportable relationship with the divine. How this relationship is achieved cannot be deduced from Hölderlin's poem, given our general considerations of the reference of texts to each other. The mention of Rousseau and his text is necessary in that Rousseau's text is not appropriated but continues to speak in its own name. I therefore assume that Rousseau's text enables an understanding of Hölderlin's text otherwise not possible. How the relationship to the divine is mastered is not explained in Hölderlin's poem but must be approached via Rousseau's text. But what "Rousseau's text" means is now limited in that I have tried to understand it by way of guidelines found in Hölderlin's poem. The most important clue is provided in the verse "Dann scheint ihm oft das Beste" (v. 159) and precludes a simple reading for content. Overcoming the fear of divine onus is not achieved during Rousseau's stay at Lake Bienne but in thinking back on it, that is, in the state of mind that created the Fifth Walk. This overcoming is neither final nor singular. The word *often* makes it impossible to relate the singular biographical occurrence of Rousseau's sojourn on St. Peter's. Much more important is the repeatable realization of this remembered singularity. The entire development described in three stanzas about Rousseau, if we pay attention to the word *often*, is not meant as an irreversible progression leading to a determined goal. The divine can always become a danger, and if mortal humans are frightened, it always seems best to be at Lake Bienne. Rousseau's text is set in the exemplary course as an exemplary means of overcoming the fear of the divine onus. We are then faced with the task of understanding Rousseau's text based on Hölderlin's guidance as a way to carry the burden of the divine.

It seems at first difficult to make a connection between our interpretation carried out according to Hölderlin's guidance and the Rhine hymn. The second half of the eleventh stanza does not at first seem to allow any connection to what Rousseau expresses about the relationship of the speaker to what he says. The main points of this passage seem instead to indicate that Hölderlin refers to content and interprets this in a particular way. The passage has usually been read so that the one subjected to, then frightened by, the divine burden withdraws to a place where he is no longer directly affected by the divine. The word *vergessen* (v. 160), to be read as active (Böschenstein, 104), points to flight and search for asylum from the divine and means having forgotten rather than being forgotten. Sleep (v. 166), too, seems to guarantee peace from anxiety, and the phrase "Where the beam does not sear" (v. 161) can, in Hölderlin's language, only mean the place where one is spared the merciless directness of divine presence. How this withdrawal is to be understood is, in the framework of this reading, less important than the conclusion that it cannot be Rousseau's stay on Lake Bienne. The word *often* provides the act with a repeatability not befitting the event but only its linguistic representation. This means that Hölderlin's Rousseau does not retreat to St. Peter's but to a special way of speaking about this event. This discourse must, if it is a flight from a danger that threatens the speaker at the time of speaking, be so insistent in what it says that everything else is forgotten. This kind of discourse is nostalgic narration, mentioned in connection with Rousseau's text. It strives to achieve such a complete realization of the narrative that its language is forgotten, enabling the event's repetition. This interpretation of Rousseau's retreat as an escape into the forgetting of language is unsatisfying for both texts in several respects. The realization, gained in anxiety, has in this escape by no means been overcome, only repressed. The flight, occurring as the discourse, would be naive but without divine sanction. We would also not expect an escape to somehow introduce an opportunity for a more tolerable relationship with the divine. Escape would be the negation of the inclination to face up to it. Coming from Rousseau, reduction to a language-forgetting discourse would be untenable as well. It does come up in the Fifth Walk, not as an actual devotion to the narrative, but reflected as language's potential to entice us into what it expresses. But even if Hölderlin's Rousseau could be completely transferred to a referential illusion, he would not escape the divine, because the condition in which he would be placed would be divine. It is hard to believe that Hölderlin overlooked one of the few passages in Rousseau's text where the theme of his own poem comes to bear, even if in a very different way: "as long as this state lasts, we are self-sufficient like God" (1047). Finally, the complex relationship between the narrator and the narrative is emphasized and discussed too much at the end of the Fifth Walk to be limited to a simple flight into what is expressed. On the other hand, there is nothing in the Hölderlin passage referring to the Fifth Walk that could be connected to Rousseau's thoughts on the relationship between discourse and what it expresses. This changes if we include the broader context of Hölderlin's poem.

The clearest mention of the relationship between the divine and the human, shared by the Rousseau passage, is in the eighth stanza.

> Es haben aber an eigner
> Unsterblichkeit die Götter genug, und bedürfen
> Die Himmlischen eines Dings,
> So sinds Heroën und Menschen

Und Sterbliche sonst. Denn weil
Die Seeligsten nichts fühlen von selbst,
Muss wohl, wenn solches zu sagen
Erlaubt ist, in der Götter Nahmen
Theilnehmend fühlen ein Andrer,
Den brauchen sie; (Vv. 105–14)

But their own immortality
Suffices the gods, and if
The Heavenly have need of one thing,
It is of heroes and human beings
And other mortals. For since
The most Blessed in themselves feel nothing
Another, if to say such a thing is
Permitted, must, I suppose,
Vicariously feel in the name of the gods,
And in him they need;

There exists an earlier, rejected version:

Denn irrlos gehn, geradeblikend die	105
Vom Anfang an zum vorbestimmten End'	106
Und immer siegerisch und immerhin ist gleich	107
Die That und der Wille bei diesen.	108
Drum fühlen es die Seeligen selbst nicht,	109
Doch ihre Freude ist	110
Die Sag und die Rede der Menschen.	111

(2, 726, vv. 22–28)

For they travel aimlessly, gazing straight ahead	105
From beginning to predetermined end	106
And always victorious and the same	107
Are deed and will for them.	108
The blessed do not, therefore, feel themselves,	109
Their joy is, rather,	110
The narrative and discourse of mortals.	111

These verses reflect Hölderlin's thinking going back to his first encounter with Fichte's philosophy and continued in the Hom-

burger Essays. In a letter to Hegel dated January 26, 1795, Hölderlin discusses Fichte's absolute I, which contains all reality:

> It is everything, and outside it is nothing; there is, then, no object for
> this absolute I, for otherwise there would be no reality within it; a
> consciousness without object is, however, unthinkable, and if I myself
> am this object, then I am, as such, necessarily limited, even if it is only
> a temporal limitation, that is, not absolute; there is, therefore, no
> consciousness possible in the absolute I; as absolute I, I have no
> consciousness, and insofar as I have no consciousness, I am (for
> myself) nothing; therefore, the absolute I is (for myself) nothing. (6,
> 155)

Hölderlin, and this is meant as a criticism of Fichte, can only
imagine the absolute as the unconscious, because it can have no
object outside itself. The absolute I is in itself nothing because,
having a consciousness of itself and being object to itself, it would
no longer be absolute. To have a consciousness of the perfect, there
must be imperfection. This is also substantiated by the beginning
of the fragment *Hyperions Jugend* (Hyperion's youth), where the
concept of self-perception is introduced.

> If we were once perfect and free of all limitations, we would not have
> lost our all-encompassing sufficiency, the right of all pure spirits, for
> nothing. We traded the feeling for life, the bright consciousness for the
> carefree rest of the gods. Just think, if you can, of the pure spirit! It
> does not concern itself with matter; that is why no world is alive for it;
> no sun rises or sets for it; it is everything and therefore is nothing for
> itself. It does not go without, because it cannot desire; it does not
> suffer, because it does not live.—Forgive me the thought! it is only
> thought and nothing else.—Now we sense the limits of our existence,
> and the restrained power wrestles anxiously with its bonds, and the
> spirit yearns for the clear ether. But there is something in us that gladly
> endures these bonds; for if the spirit were unlimited by any resistance,
> we would be unaware of ourselves and others. To not be aware of
> oneself is death. (3, 201f.)

All these texts speak to the paradox of the imperfection of the
perfect, which, in that it is everything and outside itself nothing,

is denied the opportunity to compare itself with others and recognize itself as perfect. To be sensed, the perfect must have within itself the drive to create the imperfect. This must not be experienced by the perfect as something outside itself, because perfection would be negated as soon as something were to be assumed outside it. The perfect must therefore create imperfection within itself. It should be separate but at the same time be part of it. In his essay "Über den Unterschied der Dichtarten" (On distinctions of poetics), Hölderlin conceives of the creation of the imperfect out of perfection as the process of dividing the whole into its parts. The part is, inside the whole, separate and thereby the means for the whole to become aware of itself without sacrificing its perfection. It is reasonable to ask, however, how the whole, complete unto itself, can initiate the process of division, since it could stay at rest in its perfection. Hölderlin speaks of an "excess of spirit in unity" (4, 269). There is something beyond the whole, an augmentation, that initiates the division of the whole into its parts. Hölderlin calls it "the necessary discretion of Zeus" (4, 269). Zeus represents a play on the division of the whole as creative act. This act is capricious because the whole in its perfection is not determined by anything and can only act freely out of itself. Nevertheless, this free act is necessary because only through it, that is, through the creation of imperfection, can the whole become aware of its perfection. The whole can only come to itself in that it goes out of itself. The necessary discretion of Zeus is, within the whole, more than the whole that makes it spill over. This overflow limits the imperfect in its parts as it strives to regain perfection in the unified whole and, in the sense of its imperfect partition, senses the perfection of the whole in which it takes part but which it is not.

In the Rhine hymn, the relationship between the whole and the part appears as the relationship between God and mankind. God needs mankind to sense in His name what He cannot feel Himself. Based on the many passages that demonstrate Hölderlin's effort to come to grips with this relationship, it is impossible to understand the relationship as complementary. God is not in need of mankind in the same way that imperfection is in need of what it lacks to become faultless perfection. Mankind is not the complement to God, because He has always been perfect. God does not need mankind because He is lacking something but because of His perfection, which makes it impossible for Him to sense His own perfection. Human perception in the name of God does not fill a void but is added to the perfect as an extension, which seems to be superfluous from the viewpoint of the perfection of what is felt but seems necessary based on the inability of the perfect to be aware of itself. Necessary excess is the foundation without which none of Hölderlin's attempts to understand the sensibility of the divine can stand. The necessary discretion of Zeus and the participating feeling of mankind are both this augmentation, without which the perfection of the perfect could not appear and of which it is therefore both dependent and independent. Necessary discretion is the augmentation seen from above: the excess of the whole, the reason for its division and encounter with itself in its own parts. Human awareness and discourse is the augmentation seen from below: the addition to the perfect, imperfect only because it is felt and expressed.

The third and fourth sections of the Rhine hymn examine ways in which the relationship between mankind and God, characterized in the eighth stanza, can succeed or fail. Awareness in the name of the gods is awareness of the divine. This feeling requires that man be able to participate in place of God, who he is not. Only those who are mortal can sense it, but to do so they have to contrast immortality with their own mortality. In feeling what one is not, there is always the danger of forgetting that one is not what one feels. Those who succumb to the temptation of believing that they are only what they can feel, because they are not, are "defiant" (v. 101). They strive for divinity and lose the sense of their own imperfection. Their presumption is based on forgetting the language of feeling, which can represent the divine insofar as it is different. The contrast to the audacity of the defiant is Rousseau's fear. When the distance between the person feeling divinity and what we feel grows too small, we succumb to hubris. If the distance grows too great, then we become frightened of the immensity we are supposed to sense in our imperfection. In contrast with the audacious, who transgress against the divine and are punished, the frightened are given the chance to overcome their fright through a better understanding of their relationship to the divine. In this understanding, described in the eighth stanza, those who feel must understand themselves to be both superfluous and necessary to the divine. That they are used will save them from succumbing to their own weakness, and being superfluous will prevent them from losing themselves as godlike. Hölderlin does not directly say that Rousseau, among the frightened, attains such a balanced relationship to the divine. He does so through reference to the Fifth Walk. A connection between the two texts is now established. Hölderlin's relationship between mankind and God corresponds to Rousseau's relationship between the narrator and the narrative. Mankind's feeling is an augmentation to the perfection of God, just as narration is an augmentation to the perfection of the narrative. For Rousseau, the narrative is additionally a condition of godlike self-sufficiency that seems not to allow any experience beyond itself and is still heightened in the language of being remembered. From the narrator's insight in the Fifth Walk, his position becomes justified. What is told can be as perfect as it likes, it is still elevated by being told. If Hölderlin's Rousseau, as the narrator of the Fifth Walk, understands feeling in the name of God in this way, then this understanding conquers the fear that results from the disproportion between mankind and God and makes clear the task for which God needs him. This understanding does not belong to all who feel in the name of God but only to those who consider this feeling in retrospect. This is true in Rousseau's text, but also in Hölderlin's poem, where Rousseau seems to think it the Best to be at Lake Bienne; however, in that it seems to him the Best, it really is the Highest.

> bis in den Tod
> Kann aber ein Mensch auch
> Im Gedächtniß noch das Beste behalten,
> Und dann erlebt er das Höchste. (Vv. 199–202)

> but until death
> A mortal too can retain
> And bear in mind what is best
> And then is supremely favoured.

The augmentation of remembering as opposed to what is remembered is understanding the relationship in which those feeling in the name of God stand to God. This knowledge makes it possible to carry the "burden of joy" (v. 158), something granted only to those who are capable of attaining the Highest.

> Nur hat ein jeder sein Maas.
> Denn schwer ist zu tragen
> Das Unglük, aber schwerer das Glük. (Vv. 203–5)

> Yet each of us has his measure.
> For hard to bear
> Is misfortune, but good fortune harder.

Hölderlin grants Rousseau not only the experience of the Best but also that of the Highest. The Best is the self-forgetful sleep of nostalgic discourse, the Highest is the discourse of the Best. In a discourse of perfection where this or that excessive necessity is added, Hölderlin's Rousseau gains, as the one used in his frailty by God, the opportunity to overcome the fear of the divine burden.

This establishes a relationship between the texts of Rousseau and Hölderlin that should not go unconsidered. We should begin with the twofold relationship between the Rousseau passage in the Rhine hymn and the entire context of the poem, on the one hand, and with Rousseau's text, on the other. These two relationships must be integrated into any attempt at interpretation. This was done with a reading of the Fifth Walk, first examined according to Hölderlin's guidelines regarding the relationship of the discourse to what it expressed, and then by the definition of Hölderlin's Rousseau as a figure representative of feeling in the name of the gods. We concluded that the relationship in Hölderlin between God and a mankind that feels for God corresponds with the relationship between the narrator and his narrated memories in Rousseau. In both cases, feeling and expressing perfection are understood as an amplification of the perfect, superfluous and necessary. This correspondence makes it possible to use Rousseau's text, read with Hölderlin's guidelines, for understanding the poem and to concede to Rousseau the insight into the relationship established between mankind and God in the eighth stanza. We should ask, however, how this correspondence came about. It was neither planned nor predictable, and it would be senseless to want to force an answer. The risk that nothing of the sort would happen goes along with the attempt to establish a textual relationship. The method of determining such a relationship cannot be generalized as theory, and it is impossible to develop rules for a process of general text comparison that would guarantee success. This impossibility is predicated on the unpredictability of the reader's performance of his task as a third party. The reader has a freedom vis-à-vis the texts that these cannot take away, because they require the discourse of a third. The proposed correspondence between the texts of Hölderlin and Rousseau cannot be based on any assumed intention of Hölderlin's, even though it was made possible by certain guidelines within his poem. It is the result of my interpretation and thereby bound to it. It can especially not be based on what Hölderlin says about Rousseau. This correspondence is only established if we read the texts in a way that acknowledges tendencies that may be influenced by the other but without thus impinging on their autonomy. The relationship between Hölderlin and Rousseau is the concern of the reader, who recognizes the freedom of his own text within the framework of the other texts' potential. The reader's text is legitimized by laying out the potential of the texts and by doing so intensifies their meaning. This seems to me to exist in our case not only in the fact that Rousseau's place in the Rhine hymn becomes more accessible, but also that the determined correspondence between the two texts allows for a better understanding of the reference to the foreign text as such.

The correspondence between the two texts, required by the reference in the Rhine hymn to the Fifth Walk, is to be found in the augmentation of a perfect whole by the expression of this whole. The status of this augmentation must be determined as both superfluous and necessary. Is this not also true for the reference to Rousseau in Hölderlin's poem? If we assume that the poem is in itself a complete whole, sufficient unto itself, then the reference is unnecessary. If, however, it is necessary, then it manifests the poem's demand to be connected with the foreign text. The reference to Rousseau is, independent of how the relationship to the text is constituted, the necessary discretion of the whole, the means by which it goes beyond itself to return to itself via the foreign discourse. In referring to the other text, the poem makes known that it needs the other discourse, which feels in its name. But now we see that this necessary-superfluous augmentation to the whole, as we understand the reference to Rousseau, is at the same time what makes the two texts correspond. The reference is the call for a discourse to augment and express the whole. The augmentation to the whole is its own expression. The texts of Hölderlin and Rousseau, which determine the expression of the whole as the augmentation of the whole, qualify themselves as this augmentation with reference to the whole they express (the divine, the existential feeling). But these texts are also a whole that must be expressed without being able to express itself. This is why the text, as a perfect whole, pushes beyond itself. It has within it an excess, the reference to the other text. The text flows out in the necessary-superfluous discourse, which it needs although is not lacking. I understand my own discourse in this same way.

THE PART AND THE WHOLE

Even if the reference to the foreign text questions the poem as something complete within itself, thereby ripping apart its closure, the Rousseau passage is still a part of a whole, and we should examine the connection between the two. I would like to establish this connection with the help of the last of the three stanzas concerned with Rousseau. This stanza shows a transition from Rousseau's experiences on Lake Bienne to the universal experience of the wedding feast of mankind and the gods and occupies an intermediate position that can be interpreted from its manner of discourse.

> Und herrlich ists, aus heiligem Schlafe dann
> Erstehen und aus Waldes Kühle
> Erwachend, Abends nun
> Dem milderen Licht entgegenzugehn,
> Wenn, der die Berge gebaut
> Und den Pfad der Ströme gezeichnet,
> Nachdem er lächelnd auch
> Der Menschen geschäftiges Leben
> Das othemarme, wie Seegel
> Mit seinen Lüften gelenkt hat,
> Auch ruht und zu der Schülerin jezt,
> Der Bildner, Gutes mehr
> Denn Böses findend,
> Zur heutigen Erde der Tag sich neiget. (Vv. 166–79)

> And glorious then it is to arise once more
> From holy sleep and awakening
> From coolness of the woods, at evening
> Walk now toward the softer light
> When he who built the mountains
> And drafted the paths of the rivers,
> Having also smiling directed
> The busy lives of men,
> So short of breath, like sails,
> And filled them with his breezes,
> Reposes also, and down to his pupil
> The master craftsmen, finding
> More good than evil,
> Day now inclines to the present Earth.

The stanza has always been connected with Rousseau. There is nothing to contradict this, but, following the previous interpretation, it is no longer clear who Rousseau is: the person staying at Lake Bienne or the one thinking back on his stay. Both are possible. If we read on in the previous vein, then the awakening appears as an emergence from the linguistic amnesia resulting from the rememberer's nostalgic evocation. The sleep of remembering, from which Rousseau awakens, is holy, because this godlike state can be reexperienced. With awakening, the level of insight is achieved where the relationship to the divine becomes transparent. By recognizing themselves as superfluous but still needed, those who feel in the name of God overcome the anxiety over their relationship to the divine. They are now able to approach the milder light of God. If the stanza can be assigned without difficulty to the level of the one remembering, then there is nothing in the text that would prevent its being set on the level of what is remembered. Both the sleep and the awakening, as well as what follows, would then refer to the time spent at Lake Bienne. This possibility is not very fruitful for an understanding of the argumentative context of the poem, but it does open up a path to the problematic tone in which the stanza speaks. The stanza speaks in a curious suspension that makes it impossible to assign a place to the landscape rising out of the words. The "coolness of the woods" seems to take up the "forest's shade" at Lake Bienne, but the day has been personified as a god, which invites us to read the landscape allegorically. The "mountains" and "rivers," which are evoked here in great generalities, seem to disallow any localization. That it is nonetheless possible to integrate this landscape with place names in the previous stanza prevents a complete allegorization and preserves a sense of individuality for this unreal landscape by its association with Lake Bienne, thus thwarting its complete transition to meaning.

The stanza's suspended tone is related to its multiple referentiality. In that it can refer both to Rousseau's stay on St. Peter's and Rousseau's situation as he remembers his stay, all possibilities are not yet exhausted. These verses speak in a way that does not require a connection to Rousseau. The actions of awakening, arising, and encountering follow in subjectless indetermination. Rising from a sacred sleep is wonderful, regardless who is doing it. It is as if the figure of Rousseau fades in the milder light of evening, and his experience loosens itself from him to continue to work in a broader framework. This broader connection, to be inferred from the manner of speech, presents itself if we no longer connect the stanza with what immediately precedes it. Then we can see that many elements of the landscape that unfolds in the eleventh and twelfth stanzas are already familiar from the other landscape in which the poet sees himself at the beginning of the poem.

> Im dunkeln Epheu saß ich, an der Pforte
> Des Waldes, eben, da der goldene Mittag,
> Den Quell besuchend, herunterkam
> Von Treppen des Alpengebirgs,
> Das mir die göttlichgebaute,
> Die Burg der Himmlischen heißt
> Nach alter Meinung, wo aber
> Geheim noch manches entschieden
> Zu Menschen gelanget; von da
> vernahm ich ohne Vermuthen
> Ein Schiksaal, dann noch kaum
> War mir im warmen Schatten
> Sich manches beredend, die Seele
> Italia zu geschweift
> Und fernhin an die Küsten Moreas. (Vv. 1–15)

> Amid dark ivy I was sitting, at
> The forest's gate, just as a golden noon,
> To visit the wellspring there, came down
> From steps of the Alpine ranges
> Which, following ancient lore,
> I call the divinely built,
> The fortress of the Heavenly,
> But where, determined in secret
> Much even now reaches men; from there
> Without surmise I heard
> A destiny, for, debating
> Now this, now that in the warm shade,

My soul had hardly begun
To make for Italy
And far away for the shores of Morea.

The forest, the midday sojourn in the shade, the divinely built mountains are inescapable commonalities of both passages. This introduces a new dimension to the twelfth stanza and the Rousseau passage as a whole. If the poet's stay at the beginning of the poem corresponds to that of Rousseau on Lake Bienne, then the twelfth stanza can be connected not only to the eleventh but also to the first. In it are united two strains. The entire development of the poem since the beginning and the path of Rousseau merge in the single evening awakening. Rousseau and Hölderlin both move towards the softer light. The attribution of the verbs is suspended, because the stanza refers both to the whole of the poem and to this part of the poem. It is valid for the speaker as well as the one spoken about. This suspension of multilayered discourse is an indication that the Rousseau passage repeats the entire progression of the poem and is to be understood as its self-representation. It remains to be shown how this happens.

The situation of the poem's speaker, who appears in the first stanza as *I*, is comparable to Rousseau's. If the entire development of the poem is represented in the Rousseau passage, then it is the development of the speaker in his discourse that is meant. The *I* disappears from the discourse of the poem after the first stanza, but it is important for the desired connection that it appears again at the beginning of the Rousseau passage. The appearance of the Rousseau figure coincides with the retrospection of the speaker. Since Rousseau is introduced into the text as a speaker, this coincidence is confirmation of the view that Hölderlin sees himself in Rousseau as the speaker of his poem. If we want to understand the entire progression of the poem from the standpoint of the speaker, then we must question the connection between the two passages as the speaker refers to his own situation.

Important for the first stanza is the heretofore unnoticed fact that it is written in the past tense. The sojourn portrayed is not of the poet's present as he takes up his pen, rather it is past and remembered. The speaker relates to it as a retrospective narrator in the same way that Rousseau later looks to his sojourn on Lake Bienne. The unsuspected experience of the fate of the Rhine occurred in the past, which is why the following depiction of this fate is to be understood as a subsequent report of something previously experienced. Up to and including the ninth stanza, the poem consists of narration and reflection on the narrative. This changes in the tenth stanza:

> Halbgötter denk' ich jezt
> Und kennen muß ich die Theuern,
> Weil oft ihr Leben so
> Die sehnende Brust mir beweget. (Vv. 135–38)

> Of demigods now I think
> And I must know these dear ones
> Because so often their lives
> Move me and fill me with longing.

It has been questioned whether the *now* refers only to what follows or also to what precedes it. If we read the passage in connection with the beginning of the poem, linked by the renewed mention of the *I* which had receded, then this question seems less important than the observation that the *now* contradicts the past tense of the opening stanza. For the first time, the discourse is not directed to an other about which it reports but to its own present. Important are not only the demigods but also the relationship the speaker has to them. Hölderlin's retrospection on his own discourse is not coincidentally at the beginning of the Rousseau passage, dealing as it does with the anxious hesitation in divinely naive discourse. This parallel confirms the correspondence of the Rousseau passage to the poem's whole. The beginning of the tenth stanza is, in the entire sequence, the concern attributed to Rousseau in the eleventh stanza. The speaker knows the demigods because they often stir his heart. This *often*, which characterizes the repeatability of this realization, corresponds to the *often* in verse 159, where being at Lake

Bienne seems to Rousseau to be the Best. This *often* presumes an awareness of this recurrence. If the life of the demigods stirs the speaker's heart, then it does so in a discourse of actualization, for example, in the narration of the Rhine hymn. Now, however, the demigods are *thought*. Instead of realizing them only in language, the speaker thinks about his relationship to them. By representing this reflection, the Rousseau passage takes its place. It *is* the reflection of which it *speaks*. The speaker's reflection coincides with Rousseau's reflection, and the dual reference of the twelfth stanza becomes transparent, because the discourse that expresses Rousseau's reflection represents what it does by expressing it.

But why are demigods thought in the Rousseau passage? Rousseau is introduced as one who feels in the name of the gods. Whoever feels in the name of a god must to some extent become a god without being one, and it is not farfetched to view the person who feels this way as a demigod.

> Denn über der Erde wandeln
> Gewaltige Mächte,
> Und es ergreiffet ihr Schiksaal
> Den der es leidet und zusieht,
> Und ergreifft den Völkern das Herz.
>
> Denn alles fassen muß
> Ein Halbgott oder ein Mensch, dem Leiden nach,
> Indem er höret, allein, oder selber
> Verwandelt wird, fernahnend die Rosse des Herrn,
> (*Sonst nemlich, Vater Zeus . . .* ; 2, 226f., vv. 18–26)

> For above the earth move
> Mighty powers
> And their destiny grips
> Him who suffers it and looks on
> And grips the hearts of the peoples.
>
> For all things he must grasp,
> A demigod or a man, in the way of suffering,
> By hearing it, alone, or being transformed
> Himself, divining from afar the horses of the Lord,

Denn einsam kann
Von Himmlischen den Reichtum tragen
Nicht eins; wohl nemlich mag
Den Harnisch dehnen
           ein Halbgott, dem Höchsten aber
Ist fast zu wenig
Das Wirken   wo das Tagslicht scheinet,
Und der Mond, (*Kolomb*; 2, 244f., vv. 127–34)

For lonely not one
Can endure the wealth
Of the heavenly; for indeed
           a demigod
Can stretch the armour, but
To the Highest
Such working is almost too little
Where daylight shines
And the moon,

In the Rousseau passage, the relationship of the one feeling in the name of a god, that is, the demigod, is thought.

Reconsidering the attempts to connect the Rhine hymn and the Fifth Walk, one notices certain contradictions. Above all, the double-layered composition of the twelfth stanza just proposed is hard to reconcile with the earlier course of the investigation. If the development of Rousseau and the speaker of the hymn come together in this stanza, then the Rousseau passage can be easily incorporated in the whole as the self-characterization of the poem's progression within the poem. But it is questionable how this integration of Rousseau relates to the previously emphasized foreignness of his text, which alone justifies the reference to it. The self-characterization of Hölderlin's poem in the Rousseau stanzas is not dependent on the mention of Rousseau. Why then does it use his name and his text? Is the reference to Rousseau unnecessary, necessary, or both?

A part of the poem is the representation of the whole of the poem. The whole is blind to itself, as is God, who does not feel Himself. To be expressed as what it is, it must depend on the part that can express what it is not. But by expressing itself in its part, the whole is no longer what it expresses itself to be, because the self-expressing whole is more than the whole it expresses itself to be. As this more-than-whole, it is taken away from itself. The self-expression of the whole is a constant motion, and the self-expressing text is always open. Any attempt of the whole to express itself is an attempt to close this opening and come to rest within itself. The self-expression of the whole always takes place in the illusion of being able to reach itself in this self-expression. This is an illusion to the extent that it succeeds, because this success is added to what is expressed as the unexpressed. In Hölderlin's poem, the illusion, according to which the text could have caught up with itself, is shattered by the reference to the foreign text. In opening to the foreign, the poem abandons any hope of ever being able to express itself as a self-expressing whole. This renunciation is necessary because the whole that expresses itself always offers an excess of expression that it cannot express. What any one text cannot do for itself is possible for another. A foreign text can represent one's own text as a self-characterizing text if it represents itself. This is why Hölderlin refers not to any random text but to Rousseau's Fifth Walk. In the juxtaposition of two foreign, self-expressing texts, each is able to cure the blindness of the other to itself, because each can express the other without slipping away from itself, as must occur whenever any text expresses itself. What then, from this perspective, is the reference to Rousseau? Through him the text opens itself, in each of those parts in which it expresses itself, to a foreign text, which likewise expresses itself and thereby the other as self-expressing. If the reference to Rousseau were missing, Hölderlin's poem would say nothing else. But since the poem remains *with* this reference what it would be *without* it, the text to which Hölderlin refers is able to express his poem as self-expressing without changing it. Through the reference to Rousseau, the poem enables its own expression as self-expression without having to express itself and thereby lose itself. Rousseau's text can only express Hölderlin's as self-characterizing if the connection between the two is established. The poem cannot do this alone, because it could then never go beyond its own discourse. It must entrust itself to a foreign and then to a third text, one that reads the two and then makes the connection.

The Sacred and the Word

In his article "Hölderlin und das Wesen der Dichtung" (Hölderlin and the essence of poetry), Heidegger explains why he chooses Hölderlin to demonstrate the essence of poetry. This poet rises above all others as the "poets' poet" (*Erläuterungen*, 34). This distinguishes him from others whose work only realizes "the general essence of poetry." This general essence of poetry is valid for all poetic works, is independent of individual works, and can be brought together "in a general concept." The essence of poetry is, in their case, something that precedes each individual work and is "realized" in it, that is to say, comes to be presented. Hölderlin is the poets' poet because his poetry does not validate some otherwise valid essence of poetry but is "led by a poetic determination to write the essence of poetry itself." Poetry writing its own essence is not preprogrammed but first occurs within it and can therefore not be separated from it or generalized.

Regardless of whether this distinction justifies Hölderlin's privileged position above other poets, one problem which appears in it is characteristic of Heidegger's work on Hölderlin. The general essence of poetry, which is equally valid for all poetry and therefore detached and nonessential, can be conceptually defined and expressed. Conversely, "the essential essence of poetry," as something that only exists as it happens, is inaccessible to a conceptual approach and cannot be formulated. Writing the essence of poetry does not mean expressing it. Expression requires some distance from what should be expressed, by which the transpiring discourse is already separate from what it talks about. For Heidegger, however, the one who writes the essence of poetry is also the one who expresses it. The poets' poet is also the poet *on* poets. Heidegger expressly counters the argument that writing *on* poets is "the sign of confused introspection" and "clueless exaggeration, something late, and an end." The article as a whole considers "five key concepts of the poet on poetry." That writing on the essence of poetry is at the same time a writing *on* poetry is not self-evident. The relationship between the two is instead rather problematic. It could be that the essence of poetry is most likely written where it is not discussed. In Heidegger's writings on Hölderlin, the relationship between writing poetry and writing about poetry is fuzzy, even suppressed. Hölderlin's texts are read as if they were what they themselves express about poetry. Not taken into account is the fact that poetry on poetry can never be what it expresses about itself because it *expresses* it, just as some expression can be reduced to what it expresses. This blindness may have to do with the adherence to the untenable distinction between the poets' poet and other poets. The written essence of poetry begins to share in generalities, to the extent that it is expressed, from which Heidegger would like to keep it distinct. Poetry can only express the essence of poetry insofar as it is no longer only the result of but also the instrument to understanding. Poetry sacrifices its written essence by expressing it. Poetry makes its own essence more accessible by compromising itself. What poetry expresses as its essence is not what is written in it. The tension in which Hölderlin's poems speak is lost in Heidegger, as is apparent in his interpretation of the hymn *Wie wenn am Feiertage* (As on a holiday).

Heidegger reads the poem as "the Hymn of the Sacred" (76). Heidegger's interpretation aims at the relationship between the sacred and the word. The beginning of the third stanza deals with this relationship:

> Jezt aber tagts! Ich harrt und sah es kommen,
> Und was ich sah, das Heilige sei mein Wort. (Vv. 19–20)

> But now it dawns! I tarried and saw it coming,
> And what I saw, the Sacred should be my word.

My investigation must concentrate on these verses, but I will first attempt to examine the progression of Heidegger's interpretation of the relationship between the sacred and the word based on two sentences, the first of which determines the sacred, the second its relationship to the word. They are: "The sacred is the essence of nature" (59) and "The word is the occurrence of the sacred" (76). "The sacred is the essence of nature." What Hölderlin calls nature in this poem "reverberates in the entire poem to its final word" (52). Nature, which for Hölderlin is ubiquitous and inclusive, is not a sphere of being among others. It is what is effective as its potential. "It is never encountered anywhere within reality as a singular reality" (52), because it is present in all reality. It is therefore only accessible but not attainable through reality. As something that precedes all else, it is the unforeseeable. As the basis for all transmission, it is the immediate that eludes all transmission. This inexpressibility of nature is evident in the inappropriateness of all its names. Nature, the sacred, the spirit, the open, the immediate, the chaotic are inadequate names for something that remains unexpressed in all of them. The unexpressed is present in the expressed as the inaccessible. The essence of nature is the unapproachability of its detached ubiquity. When it is said that the sacred is the essence of nature, then this connection of two names is based on the opinion that one concept—"the sacred"—comes closer to the unapproachability of the inexpressible as the essence of nature than the other—"nature." The inappropriateness of the depleted name "nature" is emphasized in two passages (56, 58). "The sacred" identifies the essence of nature as surpassing what is present in everything real. It identifies the unapproachability of the unexpressed in the expressed. It does not identify the unapproachable essence but rather its unapproachability, and it is therefore itself an inappropriate word, because it identifies what is inappropriate for every word. The inadequacy is not the word "nature," simply needing to be replaced with one more appropriate, but rather the inadequacy of language when faced with the inexpressible.

If, however, no name is sufficient for the sacred, how then is it put into words? The following sentence provides an answer: "The word is the occurrence of the sacred." The sacred does not exist in the word by being named but by happening within it. The word in which the sacred occurs is the song that testifies to both, which Hölderlin calls "the work of the gods and of mankind" (v. 48f.). Song is not just mankind's work. Something works within it that goes beyond mankind. Song is also not the work of God, who is dependent on mankind. Song therefore testifies neither to mankind nor to God but to their inseparability. This is based in a Highest to which both God and mankind are subject and that is now put into words as the sacred. The otherwise unapproachable sacred occurs as the testimony to the inseparability of God and mankind in song. In that song is the work of both God and mankind; nature, the sacred, works as the inclusive potential of this community. The sacred is not evident as something identified in song but is identified by song as what is active and occurring within it. "The words of this song are no longer a 'hymn to' something, not the 'hymn to the poets,' not the hymn 'to' nature but rather the hymn 'of' the sacred. The sacred bestows the word and comes into this word. The word is the occurrence of the sacred" (76). At this point, Heidegger's interpretation is no longer just an attempt to understand Hölderlin's definition of song but infringes on the particular song in which the definition is given. The poem *is* now the song of which it speaks. "The word of *this* song" (my emphasis) is the occurrence of the sacred. Heidegger takes this step within the framework of explaining the *now* that opens the third stanza. This *now* does not identify any specific moment but rather the present, the moment the poem's discourse takes place. Whether this discourse can be shown to be the occurrence of the sacred depends on whether the beginning of the third stanza can be read the way Heidegger does.

The verses "But now it dawns! I tarried and saw it coming, / And what I saw, the Sacred should be my word" are cited three times and read differently each time. The first time reads daybreak as an arrival, the second time as the transmission of the sacred, and the third time as the *now*, as the presence of discourse. First Heidegger takes the daybreak as "the arrival of a previously resting nature. Dawn is nature itself in arriving" (57). The arrival comes second in the word. The end of the article questions how the sacred is put into words as the immediate without being perverted in its essence and becoming something transmitted (72). The arrival remains an arrival and is therefore never present as something accessible to transmission. In that the sacred is always put into words as the arrival, it is not named in the word but occurs within it. Third, daybreak occurs now (75) in the discourse that expresses that it is put into words. Hölderlin's poem is daybreak as the occurrence of the sacred put into words.

This interpretation, in which everything is related to the occurrence of the poem's discourse, fails to consider the temporal structure of Hölderlin's verses, whose expression belongs to three different tenses. I saw it arriving in the past, in the future the sacred should be my word, but now, in the present, it is dawn. Daybreak is the arrival of day, but the arrival that occurs in the text, or better yet, seeing this arrival, is past and precedes the present daybreak. The arrival is not the coming-into-words of the sacred, because it is an unfulfilled wish that the sacred become word. The becoming-word of what was previously seen has yet to take place. The poem speaks *now*, between the having seen and the being-word of the sacred. The presence of daybreak seems to fade in relation to Heidegger's interpretation, because it cannot receive the sight of the arrival, nor does the sacred become word in it. What's more, the relationship between these occurrences has to be newly constructed.

The daybreak makes sight possible, because only light makes things visible. Seeing before daybreak pertains only to something that does not require light to be seen. Because without light there is no sight, what is seen before things become visible can only be light itself: not the light that is already present but the light that is yet to come. The seeing that precedes the daybreak is, as a seeing in the night, the sight of light's arrival. In the specific language of the poem, what has been seen is the *it* in "it dawns." The arrival of light is daybreak, and Heidegger is right to shift this arrival into the present of the ascent of the light (57). But even if the arrival of light and daybreak were simultaneous, the sight would still remain anticipatory. It is the sight of an arrival already begun before dawn, a coming of light that precedes the becoming-light of day. If light is still absent, that is, about to arrive, then the sight of dawn occurs in the dark. Daybreak already appears in its arrival, but it is as if the "it dawns" could only be seen as long as it is absent, as if the daybreak would extinguish this sight as it occurs.

Sight is not simply lost in the presence of speech. It is present in the discourse as something remembered. The sight of dawn's arrival can be expressed because it has become removed. This is how memory justifies its intent to express the remembered: "And what I saw, the Sacred should be my word." If the distance exists now, as it is being spoken, then an identification could follow, and no delay would be required. The poet would simply speak about what he had seen earlier. But the phrase "the Sacred should be my word" should not be read simply as a demand that the sacred be expressed. Instead, the sacred should *be* the word. The word that names the sacred is not itself sacred. In that both are distinct from one another, an identification is made possible. If the sacred is to *be* the word, then the discourse on the sacred must overcome the distance that is the basis for its occurrence. The wish "the Sacred should be my word" requires the discourse to go beyond itself and become what it expresses. Expression and being should coincide. This coincidence is, as long as one is speaking, always in the future and is present in the discourse only as the aspiration to go beyond itself.

The presence of speaking is a privation of the sacred. I saw it coming, and it shall be my word. But I can only say that I saw it coming and that it should be my word because this is no longer true. In the discourse that expresses what happened and what should happen, whatever it expresses cannot, to the extent that it is expressed, occur. The verb forms of the two verses make this clear and make it impossible to set the occurrence of the sacred into the present tense of the now-speaking poem. Heidegger reads as if Hölderlin says: "the Sacred *is* my word." But even if the sentence said this, it would not solve the paradox of the discourse's self-reference; rather it would simply leave us in the dark. The phrase "the Sacred is my word" contradicts itself to the extent that "my word" identifies the discourse in which the phrase occurs. The phrase suspends what it says by saying it, because the word that expresses itself to be sacred is not. By using the subjunctive as opposed to the indicative, Hölderlin avoids the confusion of saying and being to which Heidegger falls victim. The sacred is not the word simply because someone says that the word should be sacred. The poem that speaks of song is not this song but is separated from it by the distance that makes it possible to speak about it in the first place.

Opposing this we have the fact that it is still a song that speaks of song, that the discourse is, despite everything, exactly what it says it is. The discourse that speaks about the poem is not terribly different but is itself poetry. This can only mean that the discourse does occur as what it expresses. If the previous considerations are to be tenable, then they should be more precisely defined. If the poem is not what it expresses insofar as it expresses what it is, then this does not mean that it can't be what it expresses. It only means that it is not by making itself the object of its own discourse that the poem is what it expresses. What the poem expresses itself to be only exists where it does not express itself. "Where" does not mean somewhere else in the poem but on another level of discourse, a level to which we remain excluded as long as we only pay attention to what is expressed.

The "now" identifies the presence of the poem's discourse. But the event that places this discourse in the present is daybreak. "But now it is dawn," that is, the discourse and the dawn occur at the same time. It dawns now that the discourse occurs. But daybreak is not an event independent of the discourse that coincidentally happens at the same time. The poem speaks not only in the morning but whenever it is read and each time it is dawn, because the daybreak does not simply run parallel to the discourse but occurs within it. It dawns in the poem. The discourse itself brings light. But this remains a postulate, just as the phrase "But now it is dawn" remains a simple statement as long as the linguistic dawn cannot be experienced as something actually happening. Verses 19–20 make this possible if we allow them their halting movement and do not jump ahead of the gradual pace of the statement's determination too eagerly. In the phrase "I tarried and saw it coming," there is nothing at first that permits us to understand *it* as the sacred. Even if such an equivalency can be argued retrospectively based on the next verse, it would disregard the linear wording. Hölderlin does not say that he saw the sacred coming, but that he saw *it* coming. It would be of little use to argue that *it* is indeed the sacred, since this connection is made possible by the grammatical order of the sentences. But it is important that *it* in the sentence "I tarried and saw it coming" is *not yet* the sacred, because the sacred is not yet identified. *It*, in this position—disregarding the fact, as already shown, that the *it* from "it dawns" is taken up—is the anticipation of a name that is still missing. It is a pronoun that stands for a missing noun. In this most extreme uncertainty, it is the demand for a name that determines it. This is not immediately forthcoming. In "And what I saw," the uncertainty of *it* is at first confirmed as the unnamed thing that was seen. Not until the second part of the verse is *it* identified as "the sacred." In these verses the sacred is put into words not because it is named, but because, in the progression of the discourse, the gradual arrival represents the dawning of the name. This sequence cannot be seen as a statement. It is the reservation of a taciturn discourse that opens itself as something arriving precisely there, where it reaches for the inaccessible expression.

The poem's discourse is the arrival of the sacred, not because but in spite of the fact that it expresses it. The poem is what it says in its own manner of discourse, where it says the least, in those formulations that hardly seem to contribute to the account. There is, however, a point where the level of occurrence and the level of identification coincide. Where *it* is identified as the sacred, the occurrence merges with the identification. The identification appears from this standpoint as the goal of the linguistic progression. The course of the coming-into-words peaks in the finding of a name. But if the sacred, just put into words, is the named sacred, why then doesn't it say in this moment of fulfillment: "the Sacred *is* my word"? The subjunctive "the Sacred should be my word" changes the fulfillment to a wish. As soon as the discourse's progression has achieved its goal, the discourse defers it, so as to remain motion. It must do so because the sacred only arrives in words as something not yet present in words. With naming, the distance from which it must arrive is once again decreased. Nevertheless, identification becomes unavoidable. What is put into words and arrives in the word always moves towards being named, even though it sacrifices the character of the arrival, its essence, in its identification, being fixed as an accessible object of the present. The impetus to name and the impetus towards dissolution are both effective in Hölderlin's discourse.

How are these considerations of the opening verses of the third stanza relevant to Heidegger's interpretation? The reading of the verses in two different ways has led to opposing results. If we proceed from the temporal structure of the text, then what is to be put into words and what was earlier seen as coming are not present in the speaking that *now* concerns this before and after. Memory and desire enable what can occur as a contemporary event but cannot be named to be said. Nevertheless, these verses, as the second reading has shown, are the occurrence of arrival, not as an explicit statement but as a discourse that is recognized in its slow progress as something that feels its way along but is incapable of naming. The daybreak named in the phrase "But now it dawns" is withdrawn from itself and can only occur to the extent that it does not express itself. This silent speech event cannot be named to the extent that it happens, but nevertheless it happens as the meaning of the event—the event as past or future—and allows us to establish a connection to Heidegger's interpretation, in which the poem is the occurrence of the sacred it expresses. There remains one important difference to consider. Hölderlin's text tells us through its chronological structure that it cannot be what it says insofar as it says what it is. Its event characteristics are therefore not to be gleaned from what it expresses but only from the inexplicitness of its discourse. The inner tension of Hölderlin's discourse is missing in Heidegger, who fails to recognize the special manner of discourse and, ignoring the verb forms, simply relates the expression to what was expressed. Since Hölderlin says that the sacred should be his word, his word is already the sacred. The word is, for Heidegger, what it says in that it says what it is. Heidegger's understanding of language is different from Hölderlin's, and we should question in what way his discussion of Hölderlin's poetry is influenced by this difference.

The difference between *naming* and *being* is constantly blurred in Heidegger's text. This is clear in the following passage: "Because the daybreak, easily encompassing and wonderfully ubiquitous, has now become *the only thing to say* and *is in the word*, nature 'is now awakened with a clang of arms . . .' But why must 'the sacred' *be* the word of the poet? Because the one standing 'under favorable weather' only has to *name* what he listens to with anticipation: nature" (58, my emphasis). "Being the word of the poet" is here "being in the word," and "being in the word" is "being expressed, named." The sacred is put into words by being named. "The Sacred should be my word" is for Heidegger "my word should name the Sacred." This fusion is not necessarily incompatible with Hölderlin's text and may even be suggested by the ambiguous formulation "the Sacred should be my word." But the subjunctive makes it impossible to overstate the difference between *being* and *naming*. That the word *should* be the sacred can only be said because it is not now the case. The word that demands that the sacred be the word names the sacred without being it. Whereas Hölderlin's discourse continues in this tension, Heidegger, who ignores the subjunctive, sees the named as being present on account of its being named in the discourse. The phrase "The essence of the named is uncovered in the word" (57) expresses this precisely. It is unimportant for Heidegger to distinguish between *being* and *naming*, because to him the word *named* by the word *is* in the word.

The naming of which Heidegger speaks is not signification. The name does not refer to the named as the sign to the signified, as something separate and already present. Naming means to uncover the essence of the named. This essence is not already present but only comes to be by being named. Naming therefore means: to allow the essence of the named to occur. Since this essence can only disclose itself in being named, the named demands its naming.

This is not the reproduction of something already present, but is, as Heidegger says with a word Hölderlin uses, endowment [*Stiftung*]. If the word *naming* has been previously used in the sense of a mediating expression, then this is not in Heidegger's sense, who, on the contrary, understands naming as the process in which the thing named occurs and its essence is exposed. This naming takes place beyond all semantics. It is nevertheless not wrong to mention a more everyday use of *naming*. Heidegger himself works (at least in this article) much less with the eventful expressing of Hölderlin's poem than with what is expressed in it. What is expressed is in this case the eventful expressing, but we should not equate the two. By substituting the expressed event for the event of expression, Heidegger misses the tension of Hölderlin's discourse, which constantly speaks with the awareness that it estranges its own realization by expressing it. It can only express itself—in the everyday sense of naming—if it steps outside itself and confronts itself. Through the silent equation of the expressed discourse with the discourse itself, Heidegger confuses the endowing with the mediating kind of naming. The difficulty lies less in the unclear distinction between the two than with the fact that Heidegger is unwilling to grant the mediating naming any part in Hölderlin's discourse, whereas he himself is constantly forced to refer to the expression of this discourse, that is, to what is mediated by it. This problem can be examined more closely in Heidegger's comments on Hölderlin's fragment *Das Höchste* (The highest), which comments on Pindar.

In connection with Hölderlin's reflections on the inaccessibility of the immediate, Heidegger says: "The immediate ubiquity is the mediation for everything conveyed, that is, for the mediate. The immediate is itself never a mediate, although the immediate is, strictly speaking, the mediation, that is, the mediateness of the mediate, because it enables it with its own essence" (62). Nature affirms itself here as the place where all reality appears and in which it takes part. It "mediates appearances for everything" (62). As the unmediated enabling of all mediation, nature is the immediate. It is said of the immediate that it is the mediateness of the mediate; of the mediate that it is the mediated. In that the mediateness of the mediate is understood as its being mediated, then the immediate is equated with mediation. This equation is the special point of Heidegger's considerations (de Man, 814). The immediate is not only the enabling of mediation but the mediation itself. The distinction between the act and its enabling is thereby eliminated. This means that the act of mediation is self-enabling. If the immediate is the mediation, then there is no preceding opportunity for mediation from which the mediation could be undertaken. The immediate instead exists only as the mediation. The mediation is the occurrence of the immediate. The immediate is, however, by no means what is mediated through this mediation. "The immediate is itself never a mediate." The immediate cannot be mediated but occurs as the mediation of the mediate.

Heidegger's interpretation of Hölderlin's phrase "the Sacred should be my word" must be seen within the framework of this reflection on the immediate. The phrase reads in Heidegger's version: "The word is the occurrence of the Sacred." The sacred as the immediate that makes possible the mediation through the word cannot be separated from the word as mediation but occurs as the mediation through the word. The equation of the immediate and mediation allows Heidegger to say: the sacred is the word. The sacred is the word, just as the immediate is the mediation. But just as the immediate as mediation is never the mediated, the sacred is never what the word says but only the linguistic occurrence of what is said. The sacred occurs in the expression of another as what remains unexpressed in this expression. In the sentence "the Sacred should be my word," the event is not expressed as a contemporary event but as a desire. By expressing the event as something that should be, Hölderlin contrasts his current discourse, to the extent that Heidegger's interpretation is correct, with the word that would be the occurrence of the sacred. The discourse that is not the event but only expresses it, however, is an instrumental, communicative discourse. Insofar as it expresses the desire for eventful discourse, it strives towards its own obsolescence. It opens itself to the eventful discourse by speaking of it. But in speaking about it, it is kept at a distance. In that Hölderlin speaks of the word as the occurrence of the sacred, he strives to do the impossible, that is, mediate the immediate by turning it into its opposite, the mediated. Just as the immediate is lost in its own mediation, a discourse that speaks of the word as the occurrence of the sacred is not necessarily the occurrence itself. This transfer takes place with Heidegger, who continuously attributes what Hölderlin says about the poem to the expression of the poem. It is the same transfer that takes place in the equation of the poet on the poet and of the poets' poet.

We might now see Heidegger's interpretation in a strangely scintillating connection to Hölderlin's poem. This interpretation's goal is to make the eventfulness of Hölderlin's discourse accessible. This is almost exclusively based on what is expressed, even though, according to Heidegger's interpretation, the expression of what occurs in the discourse can never become its own expression. Starting with the expression itself is justified for Heidegger by the fact that in Hölderlin's poem, song as speech event is thematized. But the conclusion that the poem is what it says about itself is completely unsupported. That the poem *is* what it *names* as its task is asserted without presenting any evidence from within the poem itself. Heidegger's attempt is contradictory insofar as he seeks the immediate that occurs in the discourse of the poem, something that cannot be mediated by language, in the expression of the poem, where it cannot exist to the extent that it is named. This does not mean that Hölderlin's discourse cannot be understood as an event in Heidegger's sense. The double-layered interpretation of the opening verses of the third stanza in Hölderlin's hymn has shown that the discourse that expresses the event can at the same time be that event only insofar as it expresses it. Since what occurs in language stops being an event when it is expressed, the event itself remains unexpressed. It occurs in the movement of the discourse that is no longer where it came from and does not yet know where it is going. This discourse speaks to find what it has to say and arrives at its destination by not being there yet. Hölderlin's discourse expresses what it is and is what it expresses. But it is not what it expresses by virtue of its expression but through the way in which it expresses itself. This is what is special about this discourse:

it expresses the event without ceasing to be it. Heidegger's equation of *being* and *naming* is not justified, because it presumes that this coincidence needs no further explanation. Hölderlin, on the other hand, achieves the simultaneity—not the correspondence—of the two from their mutual exclusivity. This tension, the outstanding characteristic of Hölderlin's discourse, has left no trace in Heidegger's text.

Reference Matter

A Note on Translations in the English Edition

Mallarmé

The translation of *A la nue accablante tu* is based on C. F. MacIntyre, *Stéphane Mallarmé: Poems* (Berkeley, 1957) but has been substantially modified; some modifications have been influenced by Robert Greer Cohn, *Toward the Poems of Mallarmé* (Berkeley, 1965). The translations from *Salut* and *L'après-midi d'un faune* are from MacIntyre. The translation of *Une dentelle s'abolit* and those from Mallarmé's correspondence are by Bridget McDonald.

Baudelaire

Many of the Baudelaire quotations are adapted from Lois Boe Hyslop and Francis E. Hyslop, Jr., trans. and eds., *Baudelaire as a Literary Critic* (University Park, Pa., 1964); others are by Bridget McDonald. The quotation from "L'art mnémonique" is from Baudelaire, *"The Painter of Modern Life" and Other Essays*, trans. Jonathan Mayne (New York: 1964). The translation of *Chacun sa chimère* (*To Every Man His Chimera*) is from Charles Baudelaire, *Paris Spleen*. Copyright © 1970 by New Directions Publishing Corporation. Translated by Louise Varèse. Reprinted by permission of New Directions Publishing Corporation.

Rimbaud

All translations from the French are by Bridget McDonald.

Hölderlin

All translations from Rousseau's *Rêveries du promeneur solitaire* are adapted from *Reveries of the Solitary Walker,* trans. Peter France (New York, 1979). Translations from Hölderlin's *Wie wenn am Feiertage* are by William Whobrey. All other Hölderlin quotations are from his *Poems and Fragments,* trans. Michael Hamburger (Cambridge, 1980).

Works Cited

Primary Works

Baudelaire, *Oeuvres complètes* I/II, Bibliothèque de la Pléiade, Paris, 1975/76.

Hölderlin, *Sämtliche Werke*, Stuttgart ed., Stuttgart, 1946ff.

Mallarmé, *Oeuvres complètes*, Bibliothèque de la Pléiade, Paris, 1945.

——, *Correspondance 1862–1871*, Paris, 1959.

Rimbaud, *Oeuvres complètes*, Bibliothèque de la Pléiade, Paris, 1954.

Rousseau, *Oeuvres complètes* I, Bibliothèque de la Pléiade, Paris, 1959.

Secondary Works

Austin, Lloyd J., "L'après-midi d'un faune, essai d'explication," *Synthèses* 258–59 (Dec. 1967–Jan. 1968): 24–35.

Böschenstein, Bernhard, *Hölderlins Rheinhymne*, Zurich, 1959.

Cohn, Robert G., *Toward the Poems of Mallarmé*, Berkeley, Calif., 1965.

de Man, Paul, "Les exégèses de Hölderlin par Martin Heidegger," *Critique* 100–101 (Sept.–Oct. 1955): 800–819.

Documents Mallarmé II, ed. C. P. Barbier, Paris, 1970.

Heidegger, Martin, *Erläuterungen zu Hölderlins Dichtung*. 4th, expanded ed., Frankfurt am Main, 1971.

——, *Hölderlins Hymnen "Germanien" und "Der Rhein."* Complete ed., vol. 39, Frankfurt am Main, 1980.

Mauron, Charles, *Mallarmé l'obscur*, Paris, 1941.
Noulet, Emilie, *Vingt poèmes de Stéphane Mallarmé*, Geneva, 1967.

NOTE   A portion of the original German version of the Baudelaire chapter was first published as "Über die Erinnerung bei Baudelaire," *Symposium* 33, no. 4 (winter 1979): 312–30. It appeared in the German edition by permission.

MERIDIAN

Crossing Aesthetics

Library of Congress
Cataloging-in-Publication Data

Frey, Hans-Jost.
[Studien über das Reden der Dichter. English]
Studies in poetic discourse : Mallarmé, Baudelaire, Rimbaud,
Hölderlin / Hans-Jost Frey ; [translated by William Whobrey ;
translations from the French and Latin by Bridget McDonald].
  p. cm. — (Meridian)
Includes bibliographical references.
ISBN 0-8047-2469-5 (cl.)
ISBN 0-8047-2600-0 (pbk.)
1. French poetry—19th century—History and criticism.
2. Hölderlin, Friedrich, 1770–1843—Criticism and
interpretation. I. Title. II. Series: Meridian (Stanford, Calif.)
PQ431.F7413 1996
841'.709—dc20   95-10585 CIP

♾ This book is printed on acid-free, recycled paper.
It was typeset in Adobe Garamond and Lithos
by Keystone Typesetting, Inc.

Original printing 1996

Last figure below indicates year of this printing:

05 04 03 02 01 00 99 98 97 96